~ The Righteous Life ~

Born on 15 October 1931 at Rameswaram in Tamil Nadu, **Dr Avul Pakir Jainulabdeen Abdul Kalam** specialized in Aeronautical Engineering from Madras Institute of Technology. Dr Kalam is one of the most distinguished scientists of India and has been awarded the Padma Bhushan (1981), the Padma Vibhushan (1990) and India's highest civilian award, the Bharat Ratna (1997).

Dr Kalam became the eleventh President of India on 25 July 2002. His focus and greatest ambition remains finding ways that will transform India into a developed nation.

Also in the same series:

Timeless Malgudi: The Very Best of R.K. Narayan
The Writer on the Hill: The Very Best of Ruskin Bond

THE VERY BEST OF
A. P. J. ABDUL
KALAM

~The Righteous Life~
selected writings and lectures

RUPA

Published by
Rupa Publications India Pvt. Ltd 2014
7/16, Ansari Road, Daryaganj
New Delhi 110002

Sales centres:
Allahabad Bengaluru Chennai
Hyderabad Jaipur Kathmandu
Kolkata Mumbai

ISBN: 978-81-291-3456-1

First impression 2014

10 9 8 7 6 5 4 3 2 1

Printed at Gopsons Papers Ltd., Noida

Contents

Where there is righteousness in the heart,
There is beauty in the character.
When there is beauty in the character,
There is harmony in the home.
When there is harmony in the home,
There is order in the nation.
When there is order in the nation,
There is peace in the world.

Introduction

Avul Pakir Jainulabdeen Abdul Kalam's life story has been written about and recorded by himself and others many times. The story of a boy from a small coastal town in south India, one of many siblings, who goes out into the wide world, excels in scientific research and mission management and finally becomes the eleventh President of India, is the quintessential Indian story of hard work, intelligence and tenacity. Yet Dr Kalam's life or his thoughts can hardly be contained in only his story. Like a stone tossed into a pond, his life has given rise to so many ripples, each growing wider, each touching other minds and other lives.

The beginning lies in a house near the Bay of Bengal, in Rameswaram, a town known throughout the country as an important pilgrimage spot for Hindus. It was not the most luxurious of homes but one filled with love and piety. Little Abdul's father was a prominent Muslim inhabitant of the island and Abdul deeply admired and respected him. In his books *Wings of Fire* and *My Journey*, he has written about his father—his faithfulness, his contemplativeness and how he helped people with his sage advice and prayers. Abdul's mother was an equally big influence on him. He describes her as busy, efficient, keeping a large household running on a limited budget yet never stinting on her love or time with him. He was, he has written, perhaps her favourite child, often allowed to rest his head on her lap when all the others had been sent to bed. From that memory of warmth came this poem:

Mother
I still remember the day when I was ten,
Sleeping on your lap to the envy of my elder brothers and sisters.

It was full moon night, my world only you knew Mother,
My Mother!
When at midnight, I woke with tears falling on my knee
You knew the pain of your child, My Mother.
Your caring hands, tenderly removing the pain
Your love, your care, your faith gave me strength,
To face the world without fear and with His strength.
We will meet again on the great Judgment Day.
My Mother!

Kalam's descriptions of growing up in Rameswaram, his teachers, his school friends, tutors, cousins and the everyday life of a small town at the time of India's Independence are some of the most interesting and poignant parts of his writing. His first job as a newspaper delivery boy, the easy coexistence of people from different religions in a town famous for its Shiva temple, the various moods of the sea and the tides have all been described by him and eventually shaped who he became.

From Rameswaram, Kalam went to Ramanathapuram, Trichi and then Madras for his higher studies, finally graduating in engineering. In all these places he had teachers who influenced him and left their mark on his mind, making him more open and confident while also opening up a new world of scientific thinking to him. The first such teacher was Iyadurai Solomon, at Schwartz High School, Ramanathapuram, of whom he writes:

In his company, I learnt that one could exercise enormous influence over the events of one's own life. Iyadurai Solomon used to say, 'To succeed in life and achieve results, you must understand and master three mighty forces—desire, belief and expectation.' ...Iyadurai Solomon was a great teacher because he instilled in all the children a sense of their own worth. Solomon raised my self-esteem to a high point and convinced me, the son of parents who had not had the benefits of education, that I too could aspire to become whatever I wished. 'With faith, you can change your destiny,' he would say.

Other teachers followed who saw the spark in the shy but bright boy in their class and took him under their wings. He has written and spoken about the importance of teachers in the development of the mind of the child and went on to become a passionate teacher himself, holding large gatherings of students, adults, even world leaders in his thrall. His vision of education and teaching goes beyond the classroom, to this:

> For enabling empowerment of the students, we need teachers who love teaching. The teacher should realize that he or she has to ignite the minds of the youth which is the most powerful resource on the earth, above the earth and under the earth. The teacher becomes a great teacher only when he or she is able to lift the average student to excellent performance by way of special teaching techniques. The conduct of the teacher inside and outside the school should become a great message to the student in shaping their career. The teacher has to fill his or her mind with great thoughts and spread the nobility in thinking and action.

While studying in Madras, Kalam had become fascinated by flying and aircraft engineering. He had set his heart on becoming an Air Force pilot. However, he narrowly missed making it, and took up a job at the Directorate of Technical Development & Production (Air) as Senior Scientific Assistant. From there, as he got involved in various defence and aeronautical projects, he was recruited by Dr Vikram Sarabhai into the Indian National Committee for Space Research (INCOSPAR), the forerunner of what would become the Indian Space Research Organisation (ISRO). Dr Sarabhai, charged with developing an indigenous space programme for the country, had drawn up a vision document to achieve this, and Kalam ended up playing a key role in this. He has written in detail about the leadership qualities he learnt from stalwarts like Dr Vikram Sarabhai, Prof. Satish Dhawan and Dr Brahm Prakash.

Some of what he learnt while leading large complicated projects is distilled here:

Anyone who has taken up the responsibility to lead a team can be successful only if he is sufficiently independent, powerful and influential in his own right to become a person to reckon with. This is perhaps also the path to individual satisfaction in life, for freedom with responsibility is the only sound basis for personal happiness. What can one do to strengthen personal freedom?... First, by building your own education and skills. Knowledge is a tangible asset...The second way is to develop a passion for personal responsibility.

At ISRO he successfully led the team that built and tested India's Satellite Launch Vehicle (SLV-3) in 1980. The project, which lasted many years, went through numerous ups and downs, including a failed launch reported widely in the media. Through it all he learnt the values of patience and fortitude when handling failure. The SLV-3 was the starting point of India's immensely successful satellite mission programme and was the foundation on which rests its current status as one of the world's leading satellite launch vehicle creators whose Polar Satellite Launch Vehicle (PSLV) has launched seventy satellites and spacecraft into a variety of orbits.

He was awarded the Padma Bhushan in 1981 and around that time was asked to take charge of the Guided Missile Development Programme at the Defence Research and Development Organisation (DRDO) by Dr Raja Ramanna. Here he went on to develop India's missile programme with the missile systems Prithvi, Trishul, Nag, Akash and Agni taking shape at this time. Teams were put in place and he writes how the process of achieving one's goal can inject energy and enthusiasm in any mission.

It has been my personal experience that the true flavour, the real fun, the continuous excitement of work lie in the process of doing it rather than in having it over and done with. To return to the four basic factors that I am convinced are involved in successful outcomes: goal-setting, positive thinking, visualizing and believing.

Agni was launched on 22 May 1989. Kalam, a great proponent of developing indigenous technologies in defence systems that would make India self reliant and independent, has long argued for the need to develop these systems. For him, these were strategic assets and not nuclear weapon systems. He has said that these afforded the country the option of developing the ability to deliver non-nuclear weapons with high precision at long ranges. It provided a viable non-nuclear option that was of great strategic importance.

As the years sped by, Kalam became more and more involved in thinking about the state of the nation. The many people he met, along with his lifelong interest in teaching, made him often consider the legacy one generation leaves behind for another. In 1991, while looking forward to his retirement and planning to open a school for underprivileged children, he started writing down his memoirs. He had always written poetry and was an avid reader from his days as a student in Madras. The book he wrote began with his childhood days and ended somewhere after the launch of Agni. Called *Wings of Fire*, it set a new benchmark in Indian publishing. Simply told and heartfelt, it continues to inspire readers across the country even today. This was to be followed by others—*Ignited Minds, India 2020, Indomitable Spirit*—in which he articulated his influences and his vision for the country.

Always a person of action rather than just words, Kalam's vision of the country went beyond handsome-sounding platitudes. He wrote about creating a scientific temper balanced with morality and spirituality among students. He spoke about ancient Indian values balanced with the need to look ahead. He articulated a vision where there was equality and progress that left behind no one in making India a self-sufficient and proud member of nations by the year 2020. His books and lectures caught the imagination of old and young. Yet he was not going to be another retired technocrat. In 1992, he took over as the Scientific Advisor to the Minister of Defence and secretary, Department of Research and Development, and continued till he was seventy. The country's highest civilian honour, the Bharat Ratna, was conferred on him in 1997. A year later, in 1998, he led the team that conducted India's second nuclear tests in Pokhran. Five nuclear tests were conducted consecutively and India became a nuclear power. In 1999, he was appointed principal scientific advisor to the government of India with the rank of a Cabinet minister. By 2001, he was enjoying a teacher's life at Anna University in Chennai. Meant to lecture a class of sixty, most of his lectures ended up in an overflowing hall with about 200 students instead.

In 2002, he was elected the eleventh President of India. His presidential years were some of the most hopeful for the people of the country. Called the 'People's President' by the press, he moved beyond the stately confines of the Rashtrapati Bhawan and travelled the length and breadth of the country, meeting students, politicians, teachers, bureaucrats, professionals from all fields, talking to them, answering their queries patiently and filling every gathering with inspiration and pride. He talked of his humble beginnings, of working with the best minds of the country in his years at ISRO and DRDO, and laid out specific programmes to bring about prosperity and connectivity to every corner of the country. In his lectures abroad, he struck a chord among international leaders when he spoke about what India can contribute to the progress of mankind. He took simple Indian values on to the world stage and left his listeners spellbound with his deep yet direct way of talking.

One of his most celebrated speeches was the one he delivered at the European Parliament at Strasbourg in 2007. He laid out a clear vision there of what India had to offer the world and went on to tell how exactly each of these goals could be achieved.

With this background, I have brought from India, a message, a message to start three important Indo-European missions which can contribute to global peace and prosperity. These missions, I am putting forth based on India's experience and the dynamics of European Union.

1. **The Evolution of Enlightened Society**—for evolving a citizen with value system and leading to a prosperous and peaceful world.

2. **Leading to Energy Independence**—A three-dimensional approach for energy choice towards realizing clean planet earth.

3. **World Knowledge Platform**—for synergizing the core competence of European Union and India in certain areas for providing solutions to critical issues like water, healthcare and capacity-building.

Through the five years of his presidency, he brought a breath of fresh air into the highest office of the land by reaching out to every section of the people. He modernized the workings of the Rashtrapati Bhavan and brought in the benefits of e-governance there. He invited people into the President's house as much as he went out to meet them all across the country. And, while doing so, he kept writing. Till date, he has written twenty-eight books that range from the autobiographical to the inspirational and the spiritual.

Now, at over eighty years of age, Dr Kalam sill keeps a punishing schedule that would put any thirty-year-old to shame. Forever on the move, he works tirelessly on realizing his pet project, PURA (Providing Urban Amenities in Rural Areas), across India. His words, as eloquent as ever, continue to inspire readers and listeners. In his book *My Journey*, he writes:

> Hard work and piety, study and learning, compassion and forgiveness—these have been the cornerstones of my life. I have now shared with the world the roots of these features. In fact, any life that has been lived to the full, when talked about with others, is a treasure house of thoughts and feelings that add lustre to the wonder that is life. In the process, if they also give my readers wings and help them to fire their dreams, I believe I would have played my small part in the scheme of life that destiny placed me in.

In *The Righteous Life*, the very best parts of his writings are brought together. Taken as a whole, they give the reader an insight into the working of a mind that is as compassionate as it is agile, as learned as it is diverse. He is, for many people, not only an inspiration, but a guiding light that shines in a world that needs voices of sanity and reason and peace now more than ever.

SECTION 1

The Journey

I was swimming in the sea,
Waves came one after the other
I was swimming and swimming to reach my destination.
But one wave, a powerful wave, overpowered me;
It took me along in its own direction,
I was pulled long and along.
When I was about to lose amidst the sea wave power,
One thought flashed to me—yes, that is courage
Courage to reach my goal, courage to defeat the powerful force and succeed;
With courage in my mind, indomitable spirit engulfed me,
With indomitable spirit in mind and action,
I regained lost confidence
I can win, win and win
Strength came back to me, overpowered the sea wave
I reached the destination, my mission.

~

Wings of Fire

I WAS BORN into a middle-class Tamil family in the island town of Rameswaram in the erstwhile Madras State. My father, Jainulabdeen, had neither much formal education nor much wealth; despite these disadvantages, he possessed great innate wisdom and a true generosity of spirit. He had an ideal helpmate in my mother, Ashiamma. I do not recall the exact number of people she fed every day, but I am quite certain that far more outsiders ate with us than all the members of our own family put together.

My parents were widely regarded as an ideal couple. My mother's lineage was the more distinguished, one of her forebears having been bestowed the title of 'Bahadur' by the British.

I was one of many children—a short boy with rather undistinguished looks, born to tall and handsome parents. We lived in our ancestral house, which was built in the middle of the nineteenth century. It was a fairly large pucca house, made of limestone and brick, on the Mosque Street in Rameswaram. My austere father used to avoid all inessential comforts and luxuries. However, all necessities were provided for, in terms of food, medicine or clothes. In fact, I would say mine was a very secure childhood, both materially and emotionally.

I normally ate with my mother, sitting on the floor of the kitchen. She would place a banana leaf before me, on which she then ladled rice and aromatic sambhar, a variety of sharp, home-made pickles and a dollop of fresh coconut chutney.

The famous Shiva temple, which made Rameswaram so sacred to pilgrims, was about a ten-minute walk from our house. Our locality was predominantly Muslim, but there were quite a few Hindu families too, living amicably with their Muslim neighbours. There was a very old mosque in our locality where my father would take me for evening prayers. I had not the faintest idea of the meaning of the Arabic prayers chanted, but I was totally convinced that they reached God. When my father came out of the mosque after the prayers, people of different religions would be sitting outside, waiting for him. Many of them offered bowls of water to my father who would dip his fingertips in them and say a prayer. This water was then carried home for invalids. I also remember people visiting our home to offer thanks after being cured. My father always smiled and asked them to thank Allah, the benevolent and merciful.

The high priest of Rameswaram temple, Pakshi Lakshmana Sastry, was a very close friend of my father's. One of the most vivid memories of my early childhood is of the two men, each in his traditional attire, discussing spiritual matters. When I was old enough to ask questions, I asked my father about the relevance of prayer. My father told me there was nothing mysterious about prayer. Rather, prayer made possible a communion of the spirit between people. 'When you pray,' he said, 'you transcend your body and become a part of the cosmos, which knows no division of wealth, age, caste, or creed.'

My father could convey complex spiritual concepts in very simple, down-to-earth Tamil. He once told me, 'In his own time, in his own place, in what he really is, and in the stage he has reached— good or bad—every human being is a specific element within the whole of the manifest divine Being. So why be afraid of difficulties, sufferings and problems? When troubles come, try to understand the relevance of your sufferings. Adversity always presents opportunities for introspection.'

'Why don't you say this to the people who come to you for help and advice?' I asked my father. He put his hands on my shoulders and looked straight into my eyes. For quite some time he said nothing, as if he was judging my capacity to comprehend his words. Then he answered in a low, deep voice. His answer filled me with a strange energy and enthusiasm: 'Whenever human beings find themselves alone, as a natural reaction, they start looking for company. Whenever they are in trouble, they look for someone to help them. Whenever they reach an impasse, they look to someone to show them the way out. Every recurrent anguish, longing, and desire finds its own special helper. For the people who come to me in distress, I am but a go-between in their effort to propitiate demonic forces with prayers and offerings. This is not a correct approach at all and should never be followed. One must understand the difference between a fear-ridden vision of destiny and the vision that enables us to seek the enemy of fulfilment within ourselves.'

I remember my father starting his day at 4 a.m. by reading the namaz before dawn. After the namaz, he used to walk down to a small coconut grove we owned, about 6 kilometres from our home. He would return, with about a dozen coconuts tied together thrown over his shoulder, and only then would he have his breakfast. This remained his routine even when he was in his late sixties.

I have throughout my life tried to emulate my father in my own world of science and technology. I have endeavoured to understand the fundamental truths revealed to me by my father, and feel convinced that there exists a divine power that can lift one up from confusion, misery, melancholy and failure, and guide one to one's true place. And once an individual severs his emotional and physical bondage, he is on the road to freedom, happiness and peace of mind.

I was about six years old when my father embarked on the project of building a wooden sailboat to take pilgrims from Rameswaram to Dhanuskodi—also called Sethukkarai—and back. He worked at building the boat on the seashore, with the help of a relative, Ahmed Jallaluddin, who later married my sister, Zohara. I watched the boat take shape. The wooden hull and bulkheads were seasoned with the heat from wood fires. My father was doing good business with the boat when, one day, a cyclone bringing winds of over 160 kilometres per hour carried away our boat, along with some of the landmass of Sethukkarai. The Pamban Bridge collapsed with a train full of passengers on it. Until then, I had only seen the beauty of the sea, now its uncontrollable energy came as a revelation to me.

By the time the boat met its untimely end, Ahmed Jallaluddin had become a close friend of mine, despite the difference in our ages. He was about fifteen years older than I and used to call me Azad.

We used to go for long walks together every evening. As we started from Mosque Street and made our way towards the sandy shores of the island, Jallaluddin and I talked mainly of spiritual matters. The atmosphere of Rameswaram, with its flocking pilgrims, was conducive to such discussion. Our first halt would be at the imposing temple of Lord Shiva. Circling around the temple with the same reverence as any pilgrim from a distant part of the country, we felt a flow of energy pass through us.

Jallaluddin would talk about God as if he had a working partnership with Him. He would present all his doubts to God as if He were standing nearby to dispose of them. I would stare at Jallaluddin and then look towards the large groups of pilgrims around the temple, taking holy dips in the sea, performing rituals and reciting prayers with a sense of respect towards the same Unknown, whom we treat as the formless Almighty. I never doubted that the prayers in the temple reached the same destination as the ones offered in our mosque. I only wondered whether Jallaluddin had any other special connection to God. Jallaluddin's schooling had been limited, principally because of his family's straitened circumstances. This may have been the reason why he always encouraged me to excel in my studies and enjoyed my success vicariously. Never did I find the slightest trace of resentment in Jallaluddin for his deprivation. Rather, he was always full of gratitude for whatever life had chosen to give him.

Incidentally, at the time I speak of, he was the only person on the entire island who could write English. He wrote letters for almost anybody in need, be they letters of application or otherwise. Nobody of my acquaintance, either in my family or in the neighbourhood even had Jallaluddin's level of education or any links of consequence with the outside world. Jallaluddin always spoke to me about educated people, of scientific discoveries, of contemporary literature, and of the achievements of medical science. It was he who made me aware of a 'brave, new world' beyond our narrow confines.

In the humble environs of my boyhood, books were a scarce commodity. By local standards, however, the personal library of STR Manickam, a former 'revolutionary' or militant nationalist, was sizeable.

He encouraged me to read all I could and I often visited his home to borrow books.

Another person who greatly influenced my boyhood was my first cousin, Samsuddin. He was the sole distributor for newspapers in Rameswaram. The newspapers would arrive at Rameswaram station by the morning train from Pamban. Samsuddin's newspaper agency was a one-man organization catering to the reading demands of the 1,000-strong literate population of Rameswaram town. These newspapers were mainly bought to keep abreast of current developments in the National Independence Movement, for astrological reference or to check the bullion rates prevailing in Madras. A few readers with a more cosmopolitan outlook would discuss Hitler, Mahatma Gandhi and Jinnah; almost all would finally flow into the mighty political current of Periyar EV Ramaswamy's movement against high-caste Hindus. *Dinamani* was the most sought after newspaper. Since reading the printed matter was beyond my capability, I had to satisfy myself with glancing at the pictures in the newspaper before Samsuddin delivered them to his customers.

The Second World War broke out in 1939, when I was eight years old. For reasons I have never been able to understand, a sudden demand for tamarind seeds erupted in the market. I used to collect the seeds and sell them to a provision shop on Mosque Street. A day's collection would fetch me the princely sum of one anna. Jallaluddin would tell me stories about the war which I would later attempt to trace in the headlines in *Dinamani*. Our area, being isolated, was completely unaffected by the war. But soon India was forced to join the Allied Forces and something like a state of emergency was declared. The first casualty came in the form of the suspension of the train halt at Rameswaram station. The newspapers now had to be bundled and thrown out from the moving train on the Rameswaram Road between Rameswaram and Dhanuskodi. That forced Samsuddin to look for a helping hand to catch the bundles and, as if naturally, I filled the slot. Samsuddin helped me earn my first wages. Half a century later, I can still feel the surge of pride in earning my own money for the first time.

Every child is born, with some inherited characteristics, into a specific socio-economic and emotional environment, and trained in certain ways by figures of authority. I inherited honesty and self-discipline from my father; from my mother, I inherited faith in goodness and deep kindness and so did my three brothers and sister. But it was the time I spent with Jallaluddin and Samsuddin that perhaps contributed most to the uniqueness of my childhood and made all the difference in my later life. The unschooled wisdom of Jallaluddin and Samsuddin was so intuitive and responsive to non-verbal messages that I can unhesitatingly attribute my subsequently manifested creativity to their company in my childhood.

~

On the whole, the small society of Rameswaram was highly stratified and very rigid in terms of the segregation of different social groups. However, my science teacher Sivasubramania Iyer, though an orthodox Brahmin with a very conservative wife, was something of a rebel. He did his best to break social barriers so that people from varying backgrounds could mingle easily. He used to spend hours with me and would say, 'Kalam, I want you to develop so that you are on par with the highly educated people of the big cities.'

One day, he invited me to his home for a meal. His wife was horrified at the idea of a Muslim boy being invited to dine in her ritually pure kitchen. She refused to serve me in her kitchen. Sivasubramania Iyer was not perturbed, nor did he get angry with his wife, but instead, served me with his own hands and sat down beside me to eat his meal. His wife watched us from behind the kitchen door. I wondered whether she had observed any difference in the way I ate rice, drank water or cleaned the floor after the meal. When I was leaving his house, Sivasubramania Iyer invited me to join him for dinner again the next weekend. Observing my hesitation, he told me not to get upset, saying, 'Once you decide to change the system, such problems have to be confronted.' When I visited his house the next week, Sivasubramania Iyer's wife took me inside her kitchen and served me food with her own hands.

Then the Second World War was over and India's freedom was

imminent. 'Indians will build their own India,' declared Gandhiji. The whole country was filled with an unprecedented optimism. I asked my father's permission to leave Rameswaram and study at the district headquarters in Ramanathapuram.

He told me as if thinking aloud, 'Abul! I know you have to go away to grow. Does the seagull not fly across the Sun, alone and without a nest? You must forego your longing for the land of your memories to move into the dwelling place of your greater desires; our love will not bind you nor will our needs hold you.' He quoted Khalil Gibran to my hesitant mother, 'Your children are not your children. They are the sons and daughters of Life's longing for itself. They come through you but not from you. You may give them your love but not your thoughts. For they have their own thoughts.'

He took me and my three brothers to the mosque and recited the prayer 'Al Fatiha' from the Holy Koran. As he put me on the train at Rameswaram station he said, 'This island may be housing your body but not your soul. Your soul dwells in the house of tomorrow which none of us at Rameswaram can visit, not even in our dreams. May God bless you, my child!'

Samsuddin and Ahmed Jallaluddin travelled with me to Ramanathapuram to enrol me in Schwartz High School, and to arrange for my boarding there. Somehow, I did not take to the new setting. The town of Ramanathapuram was a thriving, factious town of some fifty thousand people, but the coherence and harmony of Rameswaram was absent. I missed my home and grabbed every opportunity to visit Rameswaram. The pull of educational opportunities at Ramanathapuram was not strong enough to nullify the attraction of bozhi, a South Indian sweet my mother made. In fact, she used to prepare twelve distinctly different varieties of it, bringing out the flavour of every single ingredient used in the best possible combinations.

Despite my homesickness, I was determined to come to terms with the new environment because I knew my father had invested great hopes in my success. My father visualized me as a Collector in the making and I thought it my duty to realize my father's dream, although I desperately missed the familiarity, security and comforts of Rameswaram.

Jallaluddin used to speak to me about the power of positive thinking and I often recalled his words when I felt homesick or dejected. I tried hard to do as he said, which was to strive to control my thoughts and my mind and, through these, to influence my destiny. Ironically, that destiny did not lead me back to Rameswaram but, rather, swept me farther away from the home of my childhood.

Three Great Hearts Resolve a Problem

My childhood town of Rameswaram is a small island. Its highest spot is the top of a hill called Gandamadana Parvatham. Standing there, you could see the whole of Rameswaram stretched out around you—lush green coconut palms swaying everywhere, the sea in the distance and the looming gopuram of the Ramanathaswamy Temple presiding over the skyline. It was a quiet town then. The people made their living from either fishing or coconut farming, and from the tourism that occurred due to the presence of the temple. Rameswaram is one of the holiest pilgrimage spots for many Indians, and the town was almost always full of pilgrims and tourists.

The small local population consisted of mostly Hindu households, with a sprinkling of Muslims like us, and Christians too. Each community lived in healthy contentment next to the other. The divisions and vicissitudes of the outside world rarely made their way here. The daily papers brought news of upheavals and communal fault lines being drawn elsewhere, but here, life continued at its age-old, leisurely pace.

This quiet harmony had been in place for generations. My father loved to tell us the story of our great-great-grandfather, who once saved the idol of the Ramanathaswamy Temple. The story went that on a certain festival day, the vigraha, or idol, would be taken out of the sanctum sanctorum and carried in a procession around the temple precincts. The temple has a number of tanks dotting it, and the idol was taken around the periphery of these tanks too. During one such procession, in a sequence of events no one remembers clearly any more, the vigraha fell into the tank. What a calamity that was! People stood rooted in horror, imagining the wrath of the gods falling upon them very soon. One person, however, did not lose his presence of mind—my great-great-grandfather. He leapt into the tank and retrieved the idol in no time. The gratitude of the priests and other temple officials was overwhelming. Yes, he was a Muslim. And yes, caste and religious purists would be horrified at the most sacred element of the temple being handled by someone not authorized to do so, but none of these feelings were articulated. Instead, my great-great-grandfather was treated like a hero. The temple also made a proclamation that from now on, at the festival, the temple would give Mudal Marayadai to him. This was a rare honour for anyone, let alone for someone from a different religion. It meant that on each such festival day, the temple would first honour, or give marayadai to my great-great-grandfather. This tradition went on for years and years and the marayadai would be given to my father too.

This sense of harmony continued into later years. Like I have mentioned in another chapter, my father had a ferry business in which pilgrims were taken to Dhanushkodi. Our ferry service was used by the temple too.

My father was the imam of the Rameswaram mosque. He was a deeply devout man with complete and utter faith in the Koran. He inculcated all the habits of a good Muslim in his children and indeed in his entire family. For the people of the town, he was a philosopher and guide—someone they could turn to with their problems, whether spiritual or otherwise.

One of his closest friends was the priest of the Ramanathaswamy Temple, Pakshi Lakshmana Sastry. Sastrygal was not only the priest but also a very learned man, well versed in Vedic knowledge. I still remember his visage perfectly. He was always dressed in the traditional attire of a temple priest, in his dhoti and angavastram. On his head he sported the mandatory tuft of the Brahmins, the kudumi. He was one of the kindest, most gentle men I knew.

There was a third person who was as important in the spiritual life of our little community and that was Father Bodal, the priest of the lone church in the town. He was as involved in the welfare of the churchgoers of Rameswaram as my father and Sastrygal, and as concerned about the need for harmony and peace in Rameswaram.

The memory of these three learned men is still etched in my mind. I can still see them—one in his turban and imam's cloak, another in his dhoti and the third in his cassock. They met every Friday evening, at around four-thirty, and discussed matters of religion and the happenings of the town. Sometimes people came to visit them at that time with specific issues to be resolved, or the three men kept each other apprised of anything that could potentially threaten the peace among the people and together, they tried to work out ways of clearing miscommunication or scotching rumours before they assumed dangerous proportions. The fundamental requirement for peace—effective communication among sections of the people—was always kept alive by these three patriarchs. Their discussions ranged over a number of topics—the Freedom Movement that was taking the country in an entirely new direction, the attitude of the British government to the calls of the nationalists and how all this affected us, concerned them deeply. They quietly soothed the society around them, making it a harmonious whole where everyone could have an opportunity to speak freely to them.

One incident from my childhood brought this reality close to my life. I was then about eight years old, and studying in the third standard. My best friends were Ramanadha Sastry, Aravindan and Sivaprakasan. All of them were Brahmins, and Ramanadhan, in fact, was Pakshi Lakshmana Sastry's son. We led the usual life of schoolboys, spending most of the day together in the classroom and outside. Like all good friends, our day was incomplete if, at any time, one of us was absent and we could not share with each other the minute details of all that is important for boys of that age. In the classroom, we sat near one another and Ramanadhan and I shared the same bench.

Before I proceed with the main story, I would like to sketch a portrait of my school, which holds such beautiful memories of days of innocence and mischief and learning for me. It was called the Rameswaram Panchayat Primary School and I attended it from 1936 to 1944. It was situated near the seashore, and was not the most sturdy building certainly! Parts of it were built with bricks but the roof was thatched. But it was the only school in Rameswaram in those days and all the children of the town studied there. We were 400 boys and girls in total. Yes, this school had an unimpressive building and scanty amenities but it was an interesting place nonetheless. The teachers, particularly those who taught history, geography and science, were loved by the students. Why? Because they loved teaching and ensured that each one of us excelled in our studies. To give equal attention to the fifty-five children in each class could not have been an easy task. They did not want us to only earn good marks in our exams, they also wanted us to develop a love for the subjects they taught us. We saw the light of purity shining in our teachers.

Even if one student was absent for a day, they would go to the parents and enquire about the child's welfare and the reason for his not coming to school. If one of us got high marks, the teacher would be the first person to go to our homes and share the information with our parents. My school was a happy place. All of us who started our schooling there completed our studies till the eighth standard. I don't remember even a single person dropping out. These days, when I visit schools, both big and small, all across the country, I tell them that true quality does not come from a great building or great facilities or great advertisements. It happens when education is imparted with love by great teachers.

To return to my story, schools of that time, particularly small ones like mine, did not have uniforms. We were free to wear any traditional items required by our religion. My friend Ramanadhan sported a tuft, or kudumi, like his father. (Later, when he grew up, he too became the priest of the temple after his father.) I went to school wearing my little woven skullcap, like all Muslim boys of the town. Not once had any of us either noticed or remarked upon this.

When we were in the third standard, there was a great excitement in our lives—we had a new teacher at school. In a small self-contained community, this was a matter of much excitement and discussion. We students were agog with anticipation to know what our new teacher would be like. Would he be strict or lenient? Quick-tempered or patient? We could not wait for him to start teaching us. And the first day he came to the classroom, all our eagerness spilled forth.

The teacher was also a Hindu, a Brahmin. As soon as he entered the classroom, he cast a quick appraising eye over us all, perhaps taking in the diverse attire of this bunch of boys. Today, I think he must have missed noticing the bright eyes and eager smiles of the children—strangely, those are the first things that strike me when confronted by a roomful of children! But our new teacher was quick to get down to business. He walked to the front of the class and the first people his eyes settled on were Ramanadhan and I. We were the star pupils, always eager to learn and participate, and sat right in front. His eyes lingered on my cap and on Ramanadhan's tuft. A look of annoyance, even disbelief, washed over his face. Without giving any reason, he demanded to know my name. When I told him, I was peremptorily told to gather my things and move to the back row, for reasons known only to him.

I felt sad, even humiliated. I wondered why this had happened. Ramanadhan was in tears. I still recall his large eyes awash with tears as I picked up my books and moved away from him.

But neither of us was ready to let this go unreported. That very day I told my father about it, and Ramanadhan told his father too. The men were shocked and dismayed. This went against everything they had worked for! A teacher, who was supposed to be imparting knowledge and opening up our minds, was instead doing just the opposite. We had rarely seen these two mild-mannered gentlemen so agitated. They immediately spoke to one another and confirmed the details of the incident.

The next Friday, when dusk was falling, they met as usual. Father Bodal was present too. The teacher had been summoned, and presented himself. In the gathering darkness, as day turned into night, my father and Sastrygal told him in no uncertain terms that the scourge of religious divisions, which was disturbing India's fabric in other parts of the country, would not be allowed to grow here. They would not allow children to be segregated; they would certainly not tolerate anyone who made religion a divisive factor instead of being inclusive; and they would never let this infect the minds of the youngest members of the society.

All of this was conveyed to our teacher with dignity and courtesy. Would he want to see himself as a man of knowledge to whom the future of the country could be entrusted, he was asked. Our teacher stood silent, thinking. Then finally he spoke. Yes, he acknowledged, he had tried to separate the two boys. And no, he had not bothered to think through the consequences of his actions when he did so. This was the way he had seen society being structured around him always, and he was just blindly following the rules. No one had ever taught him otherwise, or made him see the futility of such divisions. He promised to rectify the wrong he had done the very next day. And he did do so.

This was how I had a first-hand experience of the way the three religious elders settled a matter firmly and openly. They made the problem go away without letting it grow and fester—the essence of good management in any situation, I later learnt.

It was also the first glimmer of a thought that has shaped me since: that it must always be our inner convictions and strength of beliefs that dictate our actions. External forces, temptations and counsels will always be dinned into us, but those among us who can stand up to what we innately believe to be good and right will finally be at peace with ourselves. Our country needs citizens who trust their individuality, who cannot be manipulated by people with unscrupulous agendas.

As far as the fact of my religion is concerned, from Rameswaram I followed my destiny that took me into the world of science and technology. I was always a believer in science, but the spiritual atmosphere of my youth has stayed with me. I well understand different points of view, particularly about God. I have read and assimilated the knowledge contained in different religious texts—from the Koran to the Gita to the Holy Bible. Together they have made me a product of this unique land of ours, a syncretic creation of the best of our diverse traditions. And if ever I am asked what it is like to be a Muslim in this country, I can point to the people I grew up with—my father, Sastrygal and Father Bodal, indeed many others like them whom I met later—who have upheld the religious and moral standards of our nation. In their own ways they have contributed to make ours a country we can justly proclaim to be a multi-religious, multi-ethnic nation, where there is space for each of us to breathe. Yes, we have deep problems and fissures being created daily, but if the generations to come remember the stories of people like my great-great-grandfather and the imam and priests of the Rameswaram of long ago, I am sure we will continue to survive and thrive as a secular democracy forever.

My Mother and My Sister

MANY YEARS ago, I wrote a poem called 'My Mother', which began with these lines:

> Sea waves, golden sand, pilgrims' faith,
> Rameswaram Mosque Street, all merge into one,
> My Mother!

My growing-up years, which I now remember with such nostalgia, are suffused with the memory of Rameswaram and the two people who were the centre of my world then—my father and mother. Ours was a middle-class family. My father had his own small business besides being the imam of the mosque. My mother, Ashiamma, came from a family, one of whom had some time in the past been given the title of 'Bahadur' by the British.

My mother was a gentle, down-to-earth, pious woman. She was a devout Muslim, like my father, and when I think of her I cannot but remember her saying her namaz five times a day, bending and praying, the look on her face one of extreme devotion and peacefulness. She had a large family to look after and that was where most of her energy went. Our family consisted of my siblings and I, as well as our relatives, like my grandparents and my uncles, all of who lived in the same house. Providing for everyone was always a stretch on the resources. It was not a time of plenty for anyone, least of all for us. We had a good steady income from my father's businesses—his coconut groves and ferry business—but that just about covered our expenses, and there was never any question about indulging in luxuries.

In these circumstances, my mother remained the ideal partner for my father. She saved and understood frugality, yet there was never a trace of irritation or anger in her about the way of life that we led.

Almost daily, not only were the many members of the family fed and looked after satisfactorily, we usually had umpteen people drop by who would be told to stay back and eat with us. Now that I think about it, I feel that she cooked and served for as many—if not more—guests as there were members of the household. Yet, this was accepted as normal, and no one really remarked on it or thought much about it. Such was the Indian concept of hospitality once upon a time.

Mine was a happy, secure childhood. One of my earliest memories is of eating with my mother, sitting on the kitchen floor. We ate off banana leaves. Rice, aromatic sambhar, home-made pickles and coconut chutney were the staple foods. Her cooking was deceptively simple and till today, I have not eaten sambhar that balances the tart and the spicy tastes as delicately as hers did. It is again in connection with food that another anecdote from my childhood comes to me.

During the Second World War years, food was being rationed and there was a general shortage of nearly everything. My mother and grandmother did their best to tide over those days, stretching the supplies as much as they could, cutting out any wastage, often reducing the portions on their plates so that the children had enough to eat. One day, my mother had made chapattis instead of rice. I sat at my place on the floor and ate with great relish as she rolled out one fresh chapatti after another. They kept coming and I kept eating. I was a hungry little boy after all. When I had finally had my fill, I picked up my banana-leaf plate and walked away to wash up. Later that night, my elder brother took me aside and scolded me for the first time. 'How could you be so blind, Abdul?' he started.

At first I had no idea why I was being pulled up. I stared uncomprehendingly at him. Then he softened and explained, 'Did you not notice that there is just enough for all of us to eat two–three chapattis each? Amma will never say no to you, but because you kept eating, she kept serving you, and tonight she will go hungry, because now there is nothing left for her to eat.'

That moment of shame, of heartbreak for my beloved mother, who looked frail, yet was the toughest woman I knew, broke my heart. I cried to myself, too mortified to show my face to anyone, and it was only after a few days that I could bring myself to look her in the face again. What a lesson that was for me to never forget the needs of those around me! Her love drove her to share her food with me without a second thought, and after my brother showed me the truth, I could never again eat without making sure there was enough to go around—especially for my mother and grandmother.

I left home fairly early in life, as I wanted to pursue my studies in a different, larger town. As a result, I could not remain my mother's little boy for too long, unlike many of my friends. But her generosity and caring spirit stayed in my heart always.

Again, during the World War II years, when I was about eight years old, I have described how I took the job of a newspaper delivery boy. My day began well before dawn, when I had to go for my tuitions, my Koran class, do my newspaper rounds, go to school and then return home well into the evening, when I had to study for the next day. In all this, my mother stood by me like a rock. Early in the morning, she would wake up well before me, draw the water for my bath and then call me. My mother saw me off and would be waiting for me to come back an hour or two later, when I would have to go with my father to the Arabic School for my Holy Koran lessons. As I went from place to place during the daytime, all I had time for were the meals that would be laid out for me promptly. I knew that many times my mother decreased her own share so that I could have enough. When I once questioned her, she only smiled and said, 'You are a growing child. You have so much to do all through the day. This is what mothers look out for, don't worry about me.' In the evenings when I returned home hungry and tired, she would again help me clean up and prepare for the next day.

Among all my siblings, I was always given precedence in taking a place by her. Once, I remember I fell asleep with my head in her lap. She sat quietly, her hands softly caressing my hair and cheeks, her touch the most precious balm for my tiredness. Unknown to me, from somewhere deep within, tears sprang up in my heart. Before I could stop them, they started flowing down. My eyes were still closed, yet the tears ran. They dropped on to my folded knees and seeped into my mother's sari. But she did not stop her caresses. She knew exactly what was giving rise to those tears—the extreme tiredness of a boy suddenly trying to be a man. Her fingers ran tenderly through my hair, comforting, soothing and understanding.

This simple lady, born and raised in a small southern Indian town, was perhaps like many other mothers in our land and beyond. She did not step out of the house and take part in the affairs of the town. She did not make a career in the way we think of it nowadays. Her realm of work remained the home and the family. Yet, within that, she served everyone and God with utmost devotion, selflessness and piety. It is this lesson that I have carried from her life—that it does not matter how large or small your sphere of activity is, what counts finally is the commitment that you bring to the job that has been ordained for you in this life.

My father lived to the age of 102. When he passed away, he left behind a family that included fifteen grandchildren. His passing away affected me deeply. I came home from my work at Thumba and sat by my mother for a long time. When I had to leave, she blessed me in a choked voice. I was in the thick of building the SLV-3 rocket, and work beckoned me. She never once asked me to stay back. Should I have done so? Should I not have been so preoccupied with my work and instead spent time with this old lady, who I was never to see again? I have asked myself this, and do not have an answer. My mother passed away soon after my father did. It was perhaps fitting that she would not live long alone, without the man whose side she had never left for over eighty years.

After I received the news of her passing, as I made my way to Rameswaram, memories of her assailed me. The two people who had created me, not just as their child, but moulded my thoughts and personality, were now no more. I would have to live out the rest of my life without their guidance. But I knew one could not have lived long without the other, and that is what comforted me as I returned to the mosque where I had learnt to pray with my father. The azaan from that mosque once used to bring all of us together—our parents leading all the children in the prayers. Now it is a sweet reminder of a beautiful childhood, of parents lost to time, of a mother who understood her boy's deepest feelings, even if they remained buried in his heart.

~

MY SISTER ZOHRA

Ours was a large family and I was one of ten siblings. Besides my own brothers and sisters, cousins and children of distant relatives were always present in the house and we grew up never knowing the meaning of boredom. There was always a tree to climb, a game to play or an excursion to plan. We were a happy bunch of children—squabbling and then making up, sometimes being naughty and always ready to help each other out.

My sister, Zohra, was one of the older children. She grew up as many girls in her circumstances did. She went to school and studied, but she was also expected to help as much as possible around the house. In fact, she was perhaps my mother's closest companion. The bond of mother and daughter changed into that of friendship as they toiled for the family, cooking and cleaning, looking after the young ones, tending to their scraped knees and dripping noses. Like my mother, she, too, had a soft spot for me. It was perhaps because I was a bit of a dreamer even then. I was not as boisterous as my companions, and often preferred to curl up with a paper or a book, rather than plan a prank with the other boys. Zohra looked out for me as much as she could so that the soft innocence of her little brother was not destroyed.

When I was quite young, a cousin called Ahmed Jallaluddin entered our lives. He came like a breath of fresh air to the tiny community. He had studied up to middle grade, could read and write English, and more than that, his vision of life was open and large, ready to look beyond the shores of Rameswaram. He stayed close by and became a part of the daily life of the family very quickly.

Jallaluddin took a great liking to me. He indulged my curiosities and did his best to find answers to the questions I asked. I was always

Into the World of Rocketry

SOME TIME in the latter half of 1962, the Indian National Committee for Space Research (INCOSPAR) took the decision to set up the Equatorial Rocket Launching Station at Thumba, a sleepy fishing village near Trivandrum (now Thiruvananthapuram) in Kerala. Dr Chitnis of the Physical Research Laboratory, Ahmedabad had spotted it as a suitable location as it was very close to the earth's magnetic equator. This was the quiet beginning of modern rocket-based research in India. The site selected at Thumba lay between the railway line and the sea coast, covering a distance of about 2.5 kilometres and measuring about 600 acres. Within this area stood a large church whose site had to be acquired. Land acquisition from private parties is always a difficult and time-consuming process, especially in densely populated places like Kerala. In addition, there was the delicate matter of acquiring a site of religious significance. The Collector of Trivandrum then, K. Madhavan Nair, executed this task in a most tactful, peaceful and expeditious manner, with the blessings and cooperation of Right Rev. Dr Pereira, who was the Bishop of Trivandrum in 1962. Soon, R.D. John, the executive engineer of the Central Public Works Department (CPWD), had transformed the entire area. The St. Mary Magdalene church housed the first office of the Thumba Space Centre. The prayer room was my first laboratory, the Bishop's room was my design and drawing office. To this day, the church is maintained in its full glory and, at present, houses the Indian Space Museum.

Very soon after this, I was asked to proceed to America for a six-month training programme on sounding rocket launching techniques, at the National Aeronautics and Space Administration (NASA) work centres. I took some time off before going abroad and went to Rameswaram. My father was very pleased to learn about the opportunity that had come my way. He took me to the mosque and organized a special namaz in thanksgiving. I could feel the power of God flowing in a circuit through my father to me and back to God; we were all under the spell of the prayer.

One of the important functions of prayer, I believe, is to act as a stimulus to creative ideas. Within the mind are all the resources required for successful living. Ideas are present in the consciousness, which when released and given scope to grow and take shape, can lead to successful events. God, our Creator, has stored within our minds and personalities great potential strength and ability. Prayer helps us to tap and develop these powers.

Ahmed Jallaluddin and Samsuddin came to see me off at Bombay airport. It was their first exposure to a big city like Bombay, just as I myself was about to have my first exposure to a mega city like New York. Jallaluddin and Samsuddin were self-reliant, positive, optimistic men who undertook their work with the assurance of success. It is from these two persons that I drew the core creative power of my mind. My sentiments could not be contained, and I could feel the mist of tears in my eyes. Then, Jallaluddin said, 'Azad, we have always loved you, and we believe in you. We shall always be proud of you,' and the intensity and purity of their faith in my capabilities broke my last defences, and tears welled up in my eyes.

My Mentor: Dr Vikram Sarabhai

TEACHERS AND mentors come at various stages into our lives. As a child, I looked up to my parents and my teachers. Then my dear friend and brother-in-law, Ahmed Jallaluddin, guided me in the crucial years when I turned from a child into a man. And, as my career was beginning, I was immensely lucky to come in the orbit of a man such as Dr Vikram Sarabhai.

A scientist, educationist, institution builder and visionary, Dr Sarabhai was one of modern India's greatest thinkers and doers. He combined an acute intelligence with the qualities of a fine leader. It was the country's good fortune that he was chosen to helm its fledgling space programme after Independence. Much has been written about him and his many achievements—that he set up the Indian Space Research Organisation (ISRO), articulated India's space mission, he was chairman of the Atomic Energy Commission and set up a number of other industries and educational institutions, not the least being the Indian Institute of Management (IIM), Ahmedabad. Yet, from where I saw him, he was all this—these were the stuff of legends and made him somewhat of a heroic figure for a young rocket engineer like me—and he was much more.

I first met him when I was called for an interview by INCOSPAR for the position of rocket engineer. The call for the interview had come to me quite unexpectedly, after Professor M.G.K. Menon of the Tata Institute of Fundamental Research (TIFR) saw my work on the Nandi hovercraft in Bangalore. I had little idea of what to expect at the interview, or who would be conducting it. Neither did I know exactly what areas of my knowledge the interviewers would test. I went to Bombay with an open mind, telling myself not to raise my expectations too much. Life had already taught me that the best way to win is to not covet the win too much; instead, to keep a calm and open mind to new challenges.

I was interviewed by Dr Sarabhai, Prof. Menon and Mr Saraf, who was the deputy secretary of the Atomic Energy Commission. Each one of them was a storehouse of scientific knowledge, yet the warmth and graciousness that I felt in the room was remarkable. That interview set the tone for my future relationship with Dr Vikram Sarabhai. He probed more into my thought processes, trying to not only find out my level of knowledge, but to know what I was made of as a person, where my goals lay and the possibilities for growth that I held within me, both as a professional and as a human being. He was encouraging, affable and listened to me in such a way that I instinctively knew that here was a man who was not recruiting just an engineer; rather, he was looking at my future potential and was investing his time and care in me. In my professional life this was the first time that I had come across someone of his stature who seemed ready to envelop my thoughts and dreams into his larger vision for the country's space programme.

I was inducted into INCOSPAR. It was like a dream come true for me, and a great career breakthrough. As I settled down into my role and got to know the institution and its processes and people, I was struck by how different it was from where I had worked earlier. The atmosphere was much more relaxed, and labels and hierarchy were not as important.

Soon after this I heard the story of how Dr Sarabhai set up the Thumba Equatorial Rocket Launching Station (TERLS). It is a story I never tire of telling, because to me it is the perfect coming together of science and spirituality—the twin driving forces of my life.

It was the year 1962 and Dr Vikram Sarabhai was looking for a site to establish a space research station. He visited a number of places. Thumba in Kerala, in southern India, was selected as it is near the equatorial region and is ideally suited for ionospheric research in the upper atmosphere, apart from the study of the atmospheric structure. When Dr Sarabhai visited Thumba, the locality had a number of villages and thousands of fishing folk were living in that area. It also had a beautiful, ancient church, the St. Mary Magdalene Church, and the Bishop's house nearby. Dr Sarabhai met many politicians and bureaucrats in order to get the place for building research facilities but it was difficult to obtain permissions. Finally, he was asked to see the Bishop of Trivandrum, Reverend Father Dr Peter Bernard Pereira. It was a Saturday when Dr Sarabhai met the bishop. The Bishop smiled and asked him to meet him the next day, Sunday. That day, after service at the church, the Bishop told the congregation, 'My children, I have a famous scientist with me who wants our church and the place I live for the work of space science research. Dear children, science seeks truth by reasoning. In one way, science and spiritualism seek the same divine blessings for doing good. My children, can we give God's abode for a scientific mission?' The church reverberated with a chorus of 'Amens' from the congregation. Subsequently, Reverend Dr Peter Bernard Pereira took the noble decision to dedicate the church building to India's national goal of establishing ISRO. That was where we set up our design centre, started the rocket assembly and designed the filament winding machine; the Bishop's house was our scientists' place. The church building has been maintained with love and care ever since and is a reminder to all of us of where the beginnings of our space programme lay. Today it houses the Indian Space Museum. Later, TERLS led to the establishment of the Vikram Sarabhai Space Centre (VSSC) and multiple space centres throughout the country.

When I think of this event, I can see how enlightened spiritual and scientific leaders work harmoniously for larger goals. Later, a new church and new schools were established in record time at Thumba. The birth of TERLS, and then VSSC, gave India the capability to design, develop and produce world-class rocket systems. India developed the capability of launching geo-synchronous, sun-synchronous and meteorology spacecraft, communication satellites and remote sensing satellites, thereby providing fast communication, weather forecasting and also locating water resources for the country. Dr Vikram Sarabhai is no longer among us, neither is Reverend Dr Peter Bernard Pereira, but I see them as flowers that blossom to bring value to others' lives. This is described in the Bhagavad Gita: 'See the flower, how generously it distributes perfume and honey. It gives to all, gives freely of its love. When its work is done, it falls away quietly. Try to be like the flower, unassuming despite all its qualities.'

This story of how we got a rocket-launching facility is an inspirational message for all generations. It is about the integration of minds. Nowhere in the world has a church been given for scientific research; it has happened only in India. It is a great message to be spread. The message is: the best component of religion can be transformed into a spiritual force that will shape society.

As I continued my work at what became ISRO, I came into contact with Dr Sarabhai more and more often. He was giving shape to his vision of the country's space programme by setting up the facility at Thumba, by conceiving the idea of India building its own SLV and, at the same time, building a Rocket-Assisted Take-Off System (RATO), which would enable military aircraft to take off even from the most hostile terrain. I would be amazed at the way his mind worked—the clear ideas and the ability to look ahead even when such things were not apparent to the rest of us.

Dr Sarabhai's leadership qualities were such that he could inspire even the junior-most person in an organization with a sense of purpose. In my opinion, there were some basic qualities that made him a great leader. Let me mention them one by one.

Firstly, he was always ready to listen. In Indian institutions, what often hinders growth is the reluctance of those at the top to listen to their juniors and subordinates. There is a belief that all decisions and ideas must come in a top-to-down manner. The line between leadership and bullying is a thin one. Dr Sarabhai amazed us often with the amount of trust he placed in us. At INCOSPAR we were essentially a bunch of young, inexperienced engineers with large quantities of zeal and enthusiasm within us. He harnessed this youthful spirit by giving us a vision and by also making us feel that we were part of a larger whole. His visits to Thumba would be preceded by days of feverish activity, as each of us wanted to show him something new that had been developed—be it a new design, a new fabrication or even a new administrative process. He groomed us to become leaders in our own rights.

A second quality that I believe stands a leader in good stead is the ability to think creatively. When Dr Sarabhai decided that we should build the SLV and the RATO, there appeared to be no immediate link between the two. Yet, time and again it was proved to us that his thoughts and tasks that initially seemed random were actually deeply interconnected. I was quick to realize this, and made up my mind early on to remain alert and focused in order to be assigned unusual and demanding tasks to be implemented at my laboratory. In the larger perspective, Dr Sarabhai envisioned India's space programme as an integrated whole, which would encompass the design and manufacture of rockets, satellites, launch vehicles and launch facilities. A wide-ranging programme for development of rocket fuels, propulsion systems, aeronautics and aerospace materials, tracking systems and instruments also gathered pace at the Space Science and Technology Centre and Physical Research Laboratory at Ahmedabad. When Dr Sarabhai gave shape to a vision to develop rockets in India, he was questioned, along with the political leadership, on the relevance of such a programme when a vast majority in the country was battling the demons of hunger and poverty. Yet, he was in agreement with Jawaharlal Nehru that India could only play a meaningful role in the affairs of the world if the country was self-reliant in every manner, and should be able to apply advanced technologies to alleviate real-life problems. Thus our space programme was never simply a desire to be one among an elite group of nations, neither was it a matter of playing catch-up with other countries. Rather, it was an expression of the need for developing indigenous capabilities in telecommunications, meteorology and education.

A third quality that I observed in Dr Sarabhai, and which I have tried to incorporate in my own way of working, was an ability to build teams. Dr Sarabhai had an uncanny knack of spotting the right person for the job. He would then back the person completely even if he or she lacked experience. He also had his own ways of raising morale—a much-required ability in a leader, particularly in a field like ours, where we often had to battle odds and failures. When required, he could make the bleakest scenario appear not so dark, he would praise us even if we had not completely reached our goal if he felt that it was justified, and he never stinted on using humour to alleviate the tensions inherent in our field. All of this helped him build teams and institutions that remained steadfastly loyal to him and his vision. Each person knew he could contribute, and that the contribution would be recognized and valued.

And finally, that great quality of his—to look beyond failures. I remember that for one of his visits to Thumba we had prepared a demonstration of the nose-cone jettisoning mechanism of the SLV stage we were working on. The plan was that when Dr Sarabhai pressed a switch, the pyro system would be activated through a timer circuit. But when he pressed the switch as requested, nothing happened. I was in a state of shock, along with my colleague Pramod Kale, who had designed and integrated the timer circuit. We quickly gauged the problem as being one within the timer, and gave direct access to the pyro after detaching it. When Dr Sarabhai pressed the switch this time, the pyros were fired and the nose cone was jettisoned, as it was supposed to. Dr Sarabhai congratulated us on our work, but there was a thoughtful look on his face as he said goodbye. That evening I was asked to meet him at the Kovalam Palace Hotel in Trivandrum. I had an uneasy feeling as I made my way there. He met me with his usual warmth and spoke about the rocket launching station. Then he turned to the incident of the morning. I readied myself to be upbraided. Instead, Dr Sarabhai delved into deeper issues—were we unenthused by the job, or was it not challenging enough for us? After talking to me, we finally came upon a reason behind that morning's failure. We needed an integrated space for the system integration of all our rocket stages and rocket systems. After pinpointing this reason, Dr Sarabhai stayed up late into the night redefining roles and coming up with a new department—the Rocket Engineering Section.

As I have mentioned, mistakes and failures are a part of every project, particularly in ones like ours where we work on a number of systems and various teams are responsible for different stages, where even a small error at one stage can put to waste years of hard work.

Dr Sarabhai used these mistakes as gateways for innovation and the development of new systems. He had the ability to look beyond the specific error and read what lay behind it. He kept room for errors and instead tried to analyse how we could make them manageable, so that we ruled the project, and not our fear of failure.

The place ISRO now has in the community of space-faring nations is second to none. It has developed world-class satellites, satellite and rocket launchers and has provided invaluable service to the country in the fields of scientific research, innovation, education and telecommunication facilities. So much so that it has sent an orbiter to the moon, the Chandrayaan 1, and will soon send a probe to Mars.* All of this grew from the seeds planted by Dr Sarabhai and nurtured by the likes of Satish Dhawan and subsequent chairmen of the organization.

My relationship with Dr Vikram Sarabhai was a deeply emotional and intellectual one. Time and again he placed his faith in me to lead teams that would design and develop mechanisms to take India further and further on her course to becoming a self-reliant nation, in terms of science and defence. He took the young rocket engineer sitting before him, answering his questions with honesty and clarity, into his fold and shared his own dream of building rockets and missiles with him. He stood by me in moments of crisis and doubt, of failure and success, guiding me, pointing me on the right path when necessary or showing me where the path lay when I was confused. He was a giant among men, and I was fortunate that I could grow in his shadow.

Dr Sarabhai's death came as a cruel blow to me, not least because it was completely unexpected. In December 1971, I spoke to him from Delhi, updating him about a missile panel meeting that I had just attended there. He was in Thumba then and asked me to meet him at Trivandrum airport after landing from Delhi, as he would be on his way to Bombay. That meeting never happened. I landed at Trivandrum a few hours later to hear the news that Dr Sarabhai had

---

*India's Mars Orbiter Spacecraft successfully entered into an orbit around planet Mars on 24 September 2014.

passed away from a cardiac arrest. I came to know that he died an hour after our conversation. The man who nurtured scientists and engineers who would go on to head important scientific projects of the country, who was a great scientist and a leader, was no more there for us to turn to. But before his going he had equipped us with the knowledge, confidence and foresight required to take on all sorts of challenges, and I believe that our greatest homage to him was for each of us to realize our own true potential, which he had spotted at the very first meeting.

It is perhaps a pattern in my life that those closest to me pass away suddenly, without warning. What has that taught me? For each person I lost I found a new layer of grief to cover myself with, and each time I tried to bring something of their essence into my own being—be it unconditional love, kindness and piety. In Dr Sarabhai's case, perhaps it was the ability to look ahead—to plan, to build and to create. If I have achieved even a part of that through my actions and through the various roles I have been entrusted with, I consider myself successful in living up to the expectations of this great visionary of India.

Teachers and Awards

On Republic Day 1990, the nation celebrated the success of its missile programme. I was conferred the Padma Vibhushan along with Dr V.S. Arunachalam. Two of my other colleagues—J.C. Bhattacharya and R.N. Agarwal—were also decorated with the Padma Shree awards. It was the first time in the history of free India that so many scientists affiliated to the same organization found their names on the awards list. Memories of the Padma Bhushan awarded a decade ago came alive. I still lived more or less as I had lived then—in a room ten feet wide and twelve feet long, furnished mainly with books, papers and a few pieces of hired furniture. The only difference was at that time, my room was in Trivandrum and now it was in Hyderabad. The mess bearer brought me my breakfast of idlis and buttermilk and smiled in silent congratulation for the award. I was touched by the recognition bestowed on me by my countrymen. A large number of scientists and engineers leave this country at the first opportunity to earn more money abroad. It is true that they definitely get greater monetary benefits, but could anything compensate for this love and respect from one's own countrymen?

I sat alone for a while in silent contemplation. The sand and shells of Rameswaram, the care of Iyadurai Solomon in Ramanathapuram, the guidance of Rev. Father Sequeira in Trichi and Prof. Pandalai in Madras, the encouragement of Dr Mediratta in Bangalore, the hovercraft ride with Prof. Menon, the pre-dawn visit to the Tilpat Range with Prof. Sarabhai, the healing touch of Dr Brahm Prakash on the day of the SLV-3 failure, the national jubilation on the SLV-3 launch, Madam Gandhi's appreciative smile, the post-SLV-3 simmering at VSSC, Dr Ramanna's faith in inviting me to the Defence Research and Defence Organisation (DRDO), the creation of RCI, Prithvi, Agni...a flood of memories swept over me. Where were all these men now? My father, Prof. Sarabhai, Dr Brahm Prakash? I wished I could meet them and share my joy with them. I felt the paternal forces of heaven and the maternal and cosmic forces of nature embrace me as parents would hug their long-lost child. I scribbled in my diary:

> Away fond thoughts, and vex my soul no more!
> Work claimed my wakeful nights, my busy days
> Albeit brought memories of Rameswaram shore
> Yet haunt my dreaming gaze!

A fortnight later, Iyer and his team celebrated the awards for the missile programme with the maiden flight of Nag. They repeated the feat again on the very next day, thus testing twice over the first Indian all-composite airframe and the propulsion system. These tests also proved the worth of the indigenous thermal batteries.

India had achieved the status of having a third generation anti-tank missile system with 'fire-and-forget' capability—on par with any state-of-the-art technology in the world. Indigenous composite technology had achieved a major milestone. The success of Nag also confirmed the efficacy of the consortium approach, which had led to the successful development of Agni.

Light Up the Sky

THE YEAR 1991 began on a very ominous note. On the night of 15 January 1991, the Gulf War broke out between Iraq and the Allied Forces led by the US. In one stroke, thanks to satellite television invading Indian skies by that time, rockets and missiles captured the imagination of the entire nation. People started discussing Scuds and Patriots in coffee houses and tea shops. Children began flying paper kites shaped like missiles, and playing war games along the lines of what they saw on American television networks. The successful test firing of the Prithvi and Trishul missiles during the course of the Gulf War was enough to make an anxious nation relax. The newspaper reports of the programmable trajectory capability of the Prithvi and Trishul guidance system, using microwave frequencies in virtually unjammable bands, created widespread awareness. The nation was quick to draw parallels between the missiles operational in the Gulf War and our own warhead carriers. A common query I encountered was whether Prithvi was superior to a Scud, whether Akash could perform like a Patriot, and so on. Hearing a 'Yes' or a 'Why not?' from me, people's faces would light up with pride and satisfaction.

The Allied Forces had a marked technological edge, as they were fielding systems built using the technologies of the eighties and nineties. Iraq was fighting with the by-and-large vintage weapon systems of the sixties and seventies.

Now, this is where the key to the modern world order lies—superiority through technology. Deprive the opponent of the latest technology and then dictate your terms in an unequal contest. When the Chinese philosopher, Sun Tzu, ruminated over 2,000 years ago that what matters in war is not decimating the enemy army physically but breaking his will so as to make him concede defeat in the mind, he seems to have visualized the domination of technology in the twentieth-century theatres of war. The missile force, coupled with the electronic warfare used in the Gulf War, was a feast for military strategic experts. It acted as a curtain-raiser for the twenty-first century war scenario with missiles and electronic and information warfare playing the lead roles.

In India, even today, the term technology, for most people, conjures up images of smoky steel mills or clanking machines. This is a rather inadequate conception of what technology denotes. The invention of the horse collar in the Middle Ages led to major changes in agricultural methods, and was as much a technological advance as the invention of the Bessemer furnace centuries later. Moreover, technology includes techniques as well as the machines that may or may not be necessary to apply them. It includes ways to make chemical reactions occur, ways to breed fish, eradicate breeds, light theatres, treat patients, teach history, fight wars, or even prevent them.

Today, most advanced technological processes are carried out far from assembly lines or open hearths. Indeed, in electronics, in space technology, in most of the new industries, relative silence and clean surroundings are characteristic, even essential. The assembly line, with the organization of armies of men, to carry out simple, routine functions is an anachronism. Our symbols of technology must change before we can keep pace with changes in technology itself. We should never forget that technology feeds on itself. Technology makes more technology possible. In fact, technological innovation consists of three stages linked together in a self-reinforcing cycle. First, there is the creative stage, with the blueprint of a feasible idea. This is made real by its practical application, and this finally ends in its diffusion through society. The process is then complete; the loop is closed when the diffusion of technology embodying the new idea in its turn helps generate new creative ideas. Today, all over the developed world, the time gap between each of the steps in this cycle has been shortened. In India, we are just progressing towards that stage—closing the loop.

After the Gulf War concluded with the victory of the technologically superior Allied Forces, over 500 scientists of the Defence Research and Development Laboratory (DRDL) and RCI gathered to discuss the issues that had emerged. I posed a question before the assembly: was technology or weapon symmetry with other nations feasible, and if so, should it be attempted? The discussion led to many more serious questions, such as, how to establish effective electronic warfare support. How to make missile development proceed apace with the development of equally necessary systems like the Light Combat Aircraft (LCA); and what were the key areas where a push would bring progress?

At the end of a lively discussion spread over three hours, the consensus emerged that there was no way to redress asymmetry in military capability except to have the same capability in specific areas as your potential opponent. The scientists vowed to achieve a reduced circular error probability (CEP) in the accuracy of Prithvi's delivery, perfecting the Ka-band guidance system for Trishul and realizing all carbon-carbon re-entry control surfaces for Agni by the end of the year. The vow was later fulfilled. The year also saw tube-launched Nag flights, and the manoeuvre of Trishul at seven metres above sea level, at speeds which exceeded three times the speed of sound. The latter was a breakthrough in the development of an indigenous ship-launched anti-sea-skimmer missile.

The same year, I received an honorary degree of Doctor of Science from the IIT, Bombay. In the citation read by Prof. B. Nag on the occasion, I was described as 'an inspiration behind the creation of a solid technological base from which India's future aerospace programmes can be launched to meet the challenges of the twenty-first century'. Well, perhaps Prof. Nag was only being polite, but I do believe that India will enter the next century with its own satellite in geo-stationary orbit 36,000 km away in space, positioned by its own launch vehicle. India will also become a missile power. Ours is a country with tremendous vitality. Even though the world may not see its full potential or feel its full power, no one dare ignore it any more.

On 15 October 1982, I turned sixty. I looked forward to retirement and planned to open a school for the less privileged children. My friend, Prof. P. Rama Rao, who was heading the Department of Science and

Technology in the government of India, even struck up a partnership with me to establish what he called the Rao-Kalam school. We were unanimous in our opinion that carrying out certain missions and reaching certain milestones, however important they may be or however impressive they might appear to be, is not all there is to life. But we had to postpone our plan as neither of us was relieved from our posts by the government of India.

It was during this period that I decided to put down my memoirs and express my observations and opinions on certain issues.

The biggest problem the Indian youth faced, I felt, was a lack of clarity of vision, a lack of direction. It was then that I decided to write about the circumstances and people who made me what I am today; the idea was not merely to pay tribute to some individuals or highlight certain aspects of my life. What I wanted to say was that no one, however poor, underprivileged or small, need feel disheartened about life. Problems are a part of life. Suffering is the essence of success. As someone said:

God has not promised
Skies always blue,
Flower-strewn pathways
All our life through;
God has not promised
Sun without rain,
Joy without sorrow,
Peace without pain.

I will not be presumptuous enough to say that my life can be a role model for anybody; but some poor child living in an obscure place, in an underprivileged social setting, may find a little solace in the way my destiny has been shaped. It could perhaps help such children liberate themselves from the bondage of their illusory backwardness and hopelessness. Irrespective of where they are right now, they should be aware that God is with them and when He is with them, who can be against them?

But God has promised
Strength for the day,
Rest for the labour
Light for the way.

~

Let the latent fire in the heart of every Indian acquire wings, and the glory of this great country light up the sky.

A Conversation[*]

A.T.: Existential issues tend to arise naturally in life, especially during transitions and intense events. They can, however, be brought forth through inner work. They arise especially as the soul learns to penetrate and transcend its ego structure. Franz Kafka wrote his celebrated *Metapmorphosis* on this theme.

A.P.J.: I can see that. The period that followed the failure of the first flight of SLV-3 and the pre-launch difficulties in Agni's first flight trial made me discover my real self in a very significant manner. But the Arakonam crash in 1999 was a devastating experience for me, also in terms of what it did to my ego-structure.

A.T.: You have never discussed that. I could only see the tip of the iceberg of the enormous pain that you have always kept submerged in the ocean of your work. Would you like to share it?

A.P.J.: More than the sharing aspect, I wish to express my gratitude to the eight young men who sacrificed their lives in a scientific endeavour. The nation must know about those unsung heroes. The pain their family suffered must be shared.

A.T.: Sir, are you talking about the Airborne Surveillance Platform (ASP) crash on 11 January 1999?

A.P.J.: Yes, the ASP crashed into the dense forests near Arakonam.

A.T.: I spoke once with K. Ramchand about this incident. He was the system engineer. He told me that the Avro aircraft, with airborne

---

*This conversation, between A.P.J. Abdul Kalam and Arun Tiwari, was recorded in the book, *Guiding Souls*.

surveillance system mounted atop as a motodome, took off around 1400 hours, climbed up to 10,000 feet and set course towards the Chennai coast. The radar testing was carried out between the Arakonam–Chennai coastline. The target aircraft for the mission trial was an AN-32 aircraft which took off fifteen minutes before the Avro. The radar performance was checked with both sea and land clutter. The performance of the radar as reported by the onboard mission crew via very high frequency communication was very good. After one-and-a-half hours of flight testing, the target aircraft landed at Arakonam around 1600 hours. Subsequently, the ASP aircraft set course from Chennai towards Arakonam and descended close to the airfield from 10,000 feet to 5,000 feet. When the aircraft was about 5 nautical miles away from the airfield at an altitude between 3,000 feet and 5,000 feet, the motodome severed away from the aircraft. The aircraft became unstable and crashed immediately at about 1620 hours, killing all the eight occupants.

A.P.J.: I was in a Defence Research Council meeting in my office in the South Block when I was told about the crash. I rushed to Bangalore to be with the bereaved families. Air Chief Marshal A.Y. Tipnis was also there. It was a very difficult moment for me, seeing the young wives crying in desperation and parents standing shell-shocked. One lady thrust her infant into my lap, saying, 'Who will look after this young life?' Another lady cried, 'Why did you do this to us, Mr Kalam?'

A.T.: Ramchand gave me the list of the officers who lost their lives. Sqn. Ldr. P. Venkataraman was piloting the aircraft. P. Ilango, instrumentation engineer, and K.P. Shaju, radar system engineer, were from the Centre for Airborne Systems (CABS); D. Narasimhaswamy, radar processing scientist, was from the Electronics Research and Development Establishment; and Sqn. Ldrs. N.V. Seshu, R. Bhatnagar and S. Ravi were the other Air Force officers.

A.P.J.: There were hardly any remains. For the comfort of the families, authorities made coffins and kept them in the community hall.

A.T.: Oh my god!

A.P.J.: In my profound grief, I could barely mumble a few words in the farewell speech I had to make. Later in the night I wrote:

The lamps are different
But the light is same.
Worldly joys you returned to the world
You remain in my innermost soul.

A.T.: It reminds me of the letter Abraham Lincoln wrote to a mother of five sons who had died gloriously in the Civil War.

I feel how weak and fruitless must be any words of mine which should attempt to beguile you from the grief of a loss so overwhelming. But I cannot refrain from tendering to you the consolation that may be found in the thanks of the Republic they tried to save.

I pray that our Heavenly Father may assuage the anguish of your bereavement, and leave you only the cherished memory of the loved and lost, and the solemn pride that must be yours, to have laid so costly a sacrifice upon the altar of freedom.

A.P.J.: The memory of the wailing widows, immobilized parents, an innocent infant in my lap and the cremation of symbolic coffins haunts me sitting here in Rashtrapati Bhavan. Do the few around going through the motions of politics and protocol understand the pain and agony people suffer out there in the laboratories and fields?

A.T.: What is the message?

A.P.J.: Don't pretend to be a candle, be a moth. Know the power hidden in serving. We seem to have got stuck with external forms of politics and mistaking them to be nation-building. It is the sacrifices, toil and valour that and seldom shown or seen that truly makes a nation.

A.T.: I understand that you had a lot of difficulty in arranging relief of about ₹700,000 for each family?

A.P.J.: I have forgotten that. There is a point at which everything becomes simple and there is no longer any question of choice, because all you have staked will be lost if you look back. Life, all through, is marked by points of no return—that is where I stood at that time.

A.T.: First time I see in you a manifestation of pain.

A.P.J.: I am sad. Are we failing our people?

A.T.: You said something similar in the Parliament recently (March 2005).

A.P.J.: Well what I said was that the arithmetical compulsions of incremental numbers and alleged tradability of certain legislative seats, won perhaps through means allegedly dubious and undemocratic, makes me feel uneasy. When politics degrades itself to political adventurism, the nation would be on the calamitous road to inevitable disaster and ruination. Let us not risk that.

Seven Turning Points of My Life

You become the captain of the problems,
Defeat the problem and succeed.

I LOVE TEACHING and research, as I never tire of repeating myself. Academic life is at the core of my thought, my innovation. Interaction with youth and their teachers is food for my inner self. I took a conscious decision to return to the academic and research area.

It was a sudden turn of events that led me to accept the presidency of the country, although I had prepared myself for a full-fledged academic career. That brings back to my memory six other events that changed the course of my life. One could add to these my re-entry into academic life in India and abroad after the presidency as a fresh transition.

~

The first turning point in my life was in 1961. I still remember, as a senior scientific assistant at the Aeronautical Development Establishment (ADE), I was the chief designer of a hovercraft. The hovercraft, called Nandi, was ready and we were demonstrating its flight to many visitors. It was a popular draw. One day, the director of the ADE, Dr Gopinath Mediratta, brought a visitor—a tall, handsome and bearded man. He asked me several questions about the machine. I was struck by the clarity of his thinking. 'Can you give me a ride in the hovercraft?' he enquired.

We took a ten-minute ride in the craft, which, in keeping with its name, hovered a few centimetres above the ground. I was piloting the vehicle, to the surprise of the visitor. He asked me a few questions about myself, thanked me for the ride and departed. But not before introducing himself—he was Prof. M.G.K. Menon, director of the Tata Institute of Fundamental Research. A week later, I received a call from the Indian Committee for Space Research to attend an interview for the post of rocket engineer.

When I went to Bombay to attend the interview, I was surprised to find Prof. Vikram Sarabhai, who was chairman of the ICSR, along with Prof. Menon and Saraf, deputy secretary of the AEC (Atomic Energy Commission), on the interview board. I was struck by Prof. Sarabhai's warmth. He did not probe my existing knowledge and skills; rather, his questions were an exploration of the possibilities I was filled with. He was looking at me as if in reference to a larger whole. The entire encounter was for me a moment of truth in which my dream was enveloped by the bigger dream of a bigger person.

The next evening, I was told about my selection. I was appointed a rocket engineer at the newly formed ISRO in 1962. This is where the greatest event in my life came about—Prof. Satish Dhawan asking me to lead India's first satellite launch vehicle programme as its project director.

~

The second turning point was my entry into India's missile programme in 1982, following my meeting with Dr Raja Ramanna at the Defence Institute of Work Study (DIWS, now Institute of Technology Management) in Mussoorie, which is an institution that trains Services officers in defence systems management, a vast area which requires some expertise. As I had been project director of the SLV-3 programme, I was asked to give a series of lectures at the DIWS. I made a presentation on how the first Indian satellite launch vehicle put Rohini into orbit. Dr Ramanna gave a lecture on how he succeeded with India's first nuclear test in 1974.

After our lectures, both of us travelled to Dehradun, where we had tea with a group of scientists. While we were at Dehradun, Dr Ramanna offered me a position of the director of the Defence Research and Development Laboratory (DRDL) in Hyderabad. The DRDL is the mother laboratory for the development of missile systems, and comes under the Defence Research and Development Organization (DRDO). I immediately accepted the offer since I had always wanted space rocket technology to be applied in missile technology. But, my next mission was to persuade my chief, Prof. Dhawan, the ISRO chairman.

Many months went by and many letters were exchanged between ISRO and DRDO and meetings were held in the Secretariat of Defence Organizations and the Department of Space to initiate a mutually convenient course of action. Dr V.S. Arunachalam, scientific advisor to the defence minister, who was then R. Venkataraman, facilitated the discussion between the minister and Prof. Dhawan. Based on these discussions, a decision was taken to appoint me director, DRDL, in February 1982.

~

In July 1992, I took over as the scientific advisor to the defence minister and secretary, Department of Defence Research and Development, from Dr Arunachalam. This was the third turning point in my life. In 1993, I was invited by Dr Chenna Reddy, then the governor of Tamil Nadu, to become the vice chancellor of Madras University. I requested the government to approve my appointment at the university, which I intended to pursue after I attained the age of sixty-two. However, the prime minister, P.V. Narasimha Rao, who was also defence minister, said that I must continue as scientific advisor as I was engaged in a number of important national programmes. I might add here that I worked with Narasimha Rao over many years. I found Rao very perceptive on defence issues, particularly on the question of building indigenous defence capability. He had a long-term vision of building robust systems for defence application. So I continued as scientific advisor to the defence minister till I was about seventy years of age.

~

The fourth turning point was the nuclear tests in 1998. There is an interesting story behind these. Let me go back to May 1996. Elections were held that year. I had met Narasimha Rao just a few days before

THE RIGHTEOUS LIFE ▪ 49

the announcement of the results. He said to me, 'Kalam, be ready with your team for the nuclear tests. I am going to Tirupati. You wait for my authorization to go ahead with the tests. The DRDO-DAE teams must be ready for action.'

His visit to Triupati was, of course, to seek God's blessings for a good result. However, the 1996 election result was quite different from what he had anticipated. The Congress tally came down sharply, to 136 seats. The BJP and its alliance came to power but only for two weeks, led by Vajpayeeji, before the third front with H.D. Deve Gowda as PM took over. However, in the two weeks that the Vajpayee government was there, it tried very hard to carry through the nuclear tests.

It was 9 o'clock at night. I got a call from 7 Race Course Road requesting that I immediately meet the new prime minister and Rao, the outgoing one. Rao asked me to brief Vajpayeeji on the details of the nuclear programme, so that a smooth handover of this important activity to the new government could take place.

About two years later, Vajpayeeji returned as PM. On 15 March 1998, around midnight, I got a phone call from Vajpayeeji. He said he was finalizing the list of ministers and wanted to induct me into his Cabinet. I told him that I needed time to think about it. He asked me to see him the next morning at 9 a.m. So, in the middle of the night, I assembled a few of my friends. We debated up to 3 a.m. whether I should join the Cabinet. The general opinion was that since I was fully involved in two missions of national importance and these were in advanced stages and nearing good results, I should not leave them and enter the political system.

The next morning I went to 7 Safdarjung Road, where the PM was staying. He received me in his drawing room and first offered me home-made sweets. I then told him, 'I and my team are busy with two important programmes. One is readying the Agni missile system and another is bringing to a close the nuclear programme through a series of tests in partnership with the DAE (Department of Atomic Energy). I feel that by involving myself full-time with these two programmes, I will be contributing more to the nation. Please permit me to continue.'

'I appreciate your feelings, go ahead, God bless you,' Vajpayeeji responded. Many things happened after that. The Agni missile system was readied for induction, five nuclear tests were conducted consecutively, and India became a nuclear-weapon state. My declining to accept the Cabinet position enabled me to contribute to two major national programmes that gave spectacular results to the nation.

~

The fifth turning point was towards the end of 1999, when I was appointed principal scientific advisor (PSA) to the government of India in the rank of a Cabinet minister. My team included Dr Y.S. Rajan, Dr M.S. Vijayaraghavan, who was a specialist in electronics and information science and had worked with me in the Technology Information, Forecasting and Assessment Council and H. Sheridon, my personal secretary who was my staff officer when I was scientific advisor. When I started this assignment, we had no office, but we built the office, thanks to the DRDO, particularly the untiring efforts of K.N. Rai, the chief executive, Civil Works and Estates of DRDO, and Major General R. Swaminathan, chief controller, R&D, at DRDO. The India 2020 vision had been accepted by the government, hence, the office of principal scientific advisor would be a good platform to push the action-oriented plans of that document, I felt. The vision was first presented during the Deve Gowda government. Following that, I.K. Gujral came in as prime minister, and then, in 1998, it was Vajpayeeji again. All three governments had pushed for implementation of the recommendations. We had an office in the Vigyan Bhavan Annexe. This is a large building with the offices of various commissions of inquiry and a few government departments. It is a quiet place. The adjoining Vigyan Bhavan, of course, is famous as a venue for large national and international conferences. The annexe is next to the vice president's residence and a good place to work away from the hustle and bustle of North and South Blocks.

As usual, travel formed a good part of my work schedule. On 30 September 2001 I had a narrow escape in a helicopter crash. The crash took place just as the helicopter was landing at the Bokaro steel plant in Jharkhand. It was a miraculous escape. As soon as I jumped out, I rushed to my pilot and co-pilot and said, 'Thank you for saving me—God bless you.' The pilots were almost in tears, but I told them these things happen, all we can do is to find out the problem and solve it. That evening I had five engagements. I had to address audiences which included officials, engineers and staff of the steel plant, and students of some of the schools of Bokaro. The news of the crash had travelled quickly. The national news channels had picked it up too. When I met the children, they seemed shaken. I shook hands with all of them and shared a hymn on courage, which cheered them. It was a simple exhortation.

> Courage to think different,
> Courage to invent,
> Courage to travel on an unexplored path
> Courage to discover the impossible,
> Courage to combat the problems and succeed,
> are the unique qualities of youth.
> As a youth of my nation,
> I will work and work with courage to achieve
> success in all the missions.

On 30 September 2001, the day I had a narrow escape in a helicopter mishap, there was the tragic air crash in which Madhav Rao Scindia and six others—journalists, his staff and crew members—were killed. These two news reports were heard by my family members at Rameswaram and my friends throughout the country and abroad. They were all extremely anxious to know how I was. I had to speak to my brother—who was not convinced by the news reports—to assure my family that everything was all right.

When I returned to Delhi later that evening, there was an urgent message from the Prime Minister's Office, requesting that I meet Vajpayeeji. He received me and enquired about the accident. He was happy to see me hale and hearty. He then told me that he had discussed the India 2020 vision document with industry leaders and the Cabinet and had made an announcement in Parliament for further action on it. But there are a number of hurdles in that action, I told him. It was something I had been thinking about.

The accident resulted in two important events. One was the seeding and birth of my book *Ignited Minds*, with the aim of inspiring the youth with the spirit of 'I can do it', and the second was my travelling from Ranchi to Quilon to meet Amma—Mata Amritanandamayee—to get myself spiritually recharged. *Ignited Minds*, as it happened, was published just before I became President. The title became a favourite phrase of the news media and occurred quite a few times in the news reports of my taking up the presidency. The book became a phenomenal success and continues to be a perennial seller. Amma is a saintly soul immersed in social welfare, specially education and healthcare, and helping orphans and destitutes. I was accompanied on this visit by two friends, and I shared with them that I had decided to resign as PSA and had sent a letter to the PM. Then I met Amma without any tension. I discussed with Amma my vision of India 2020 and value-based education.

This was in November 2001, after about two years as PSA. In my letter I said I would like to return to my academic pursuits. Of course, the reason was deeper, as I felt that programmes like PURA (Providing Urban Amenities in Rural Areas) and the management of India 2020—which I was handling—were not getting the needed priority. Where was the problem arising? As far as possible I would like to implement every goal or activity as a project with well-defined timelines, funding and responsibility. Such an environment is difficult to achieve in the overall government system when the mission objective has to be accomplished by multiple ministries and departments with their own goals and programmes. In agriculture, for example, if one sets the goal of increasing production by, say, 4 per cent every year, it would need the support of the ministries of water resources, power, fertilizers, chemicals, rural development, panchayati raj, railways (for transporting the fertilizer), and so on, and there is no clear-cut, common goal for all the contributing agencies. Secondly, the PSA's is a coordinating, advisory role with a wide sweep but no direct authority, which can be a disadvantage for mission accomplishment. This led me to take up the assignment at Anna University as professor of technology for societal transformation. This was the sixth turning point in my life.

During the last three months of my tenure as President, a question was being asked about my candidature for a second term. I had already made up my mind to go back to teaching and promoting the India 2020 vision. Suddenly, in the run-up to July, the Congress ruling party suggested some likely candidates. The opposition felt differently. The nation was buzzing with political activity and a stream of leaders from different parties came to see me, suggesting that I contest again. I received several requests from the public and eminent personalities and from the youth of the nation, both personally as well as through emails, to accept a second term. Just before the close of nominations, a team of political leaders met me and said that they would get the support of all the parties, including the ruling party, if I agreed to stand for the elections.

I told them that if most parties agreed, I would consider the possibility. The leaders came back to me and said that the ruling party did not agree to my candidature, but they insisted that I should stand for the election as they were confident of my success. Without any hesitation, I told them that if that were so, I would not stand for the election since I believed that Rashtrapati Bhavan should not be drawn into party politics. Reluctantly, the leaders agreed. A press release was issued that I would not be a candidate for the presidential elections. I took a conscious decision to go back to a career in academics and research and continue to work with passion for transforming India into an economically developed nation by the year 2020.

I have always believed that cowards never make history, history is created by people with courage and wisdom. Courage is individual, wisdom comes with experience.

'I Am a Well in This Great Land'

THERE HAS been much speculation and philosophizing about the life and times of our scientists, but not enough exploration in determining where they wanted to go and how they reached there. In sharing with you the story of my struggle to become a person, I have perhaps given you some insight into this journey. I hope it will help at least a few young people to stand up to the authoritarianism in our society. A characteristic feature of this social authoritarianism is its insidious ability to addict people to the endless pursuit of external rewards, wealth, prestige, position, promotion, approval of one's lifestyle by others, ceremonial honours, and status symbols of all kinds.

To successfully pursue these goals, they have to learn elaborate rules of etiquette and familiarize themselves with customs, traditions, protocols and so on. The youth of today must unlearn this self-defeating way of life. The culture of working only for material possessions and rewards must be discarded. When I see wealthy, powerful and learned people struggling to be at peace with themselves, I remember people like Ahmed Jallaluddin and Iyadurai Solomon. How happy they were with virtually no possessions!

> On the coast of Coromandel
> Where the earthy shells blow,
> In the middle of the sands
> Lived some really rich souls.
> One cotton lungi and half a candle—
> One old jug without a handle
> These were all the worldly possessions
> Of these kings in the middle of the sands.

How did they feel so secure without anything to fall back upon? I believe they drew sustenance from within. They relied more on the inner signals and less on the external cues that I have mentioned above. Are you aware of your inner signals? Do you trust them? Have you taken control over your life into your own hands? Take this from me, the more decisions you can make avoiding external pressures, which will constantly try to manipulate you, the better your life will be, the better your society will become. In fact, the entire nation will benefit by having strong, inward-looking people as their leaders. A citizenry that thinks for itself, a country of people who trust themselves as individuals, would be virtually immune to manipulation by any unscrupulous authority or vested interest.

Your willingness to use your own inner resources to invest in your life, especially your imagination, will bring you success. When you address a task from your own uniquely individual standpoint, you become a whole person.

Everyone on this planet is sent forth by Him to cultivate all the creative potential within us and live at peace with our own choices. We differ in the way we make our choices and evolve our destiny. Life is a difficult game. You can win only by retaining your birthright to be a person. And to retain this right, you will have to be willing to take the social or external risks involved in ignoring pressures to do things the way others say they should be done. What will you call Sivasubramania Iyer inviting me to have lunch in his kitchen? Zohara, my sister, mortgaging her gold, bangles and chains to get me into engineering college? Prof. Sponder insisting that I should sit with him in the front row for the group photograph? Making a hovercraft in a motor-garage setup? Sudhakar's courage? Dr Brahm Prakash's support? Narayanan's management? Venkataraman's vision? Arunachalam's drive? Each is an example of a strong inner strength and initiative. As Pythagoras had said twenty-five centuries ago, 'Above all things, reverence yourself.'

I am not a philosopher. I am only a man of technology. I spent all my life learning rocketry. But as I have worked with a very large cross-section of people in different organizations, I had an opportunity to understand the phenomenon of professional life in its bewildering complexity. When I look back upon what I have narrated so far, my own observations and conclusions appear as dogmatic utterances. My colleagues, associates, leaders; the complex science of rocketry; the important issues of technology management; all seem to have been dealt with in a perfunctory manner. The despair and happiness, the achievements and the failures—differing markedly in context, time, and space—all appear grouped together.

When you look down from an aircraft, people, houses, rocks, fields, trees, all appear as one homogeneous landscape, it is very difficult to distinguish one from another. What you have just read is a similar bird's-eye view of my life seen, as it were, from afar.

> My worthiness is all my doubt—
> His merit—all my fear—
> Contrasting which my quality
> Does however—appear.

This is the story of the period ending with the first *Agni* launch—life will go on. This great country will make enormous strides in all fields if we think like a united nation of 900 million people. My story—the story of the son of Jainulabdeen, who lived for over a hundred years on Mosque Street in Rameswaram island and died there; the story of a lad who sold newspapers to help his brother; the story of a pupil reared by Sivasubramania Iyer and Iyadurai Solomon; the story of a student taught by teachers like Pandalai; the story of an engineer spotted by M.G.K. Menon and groomed by the legendary Prof. Sarabhai; the story of a scientist tested by failures and setbacks; the story of a leader supported by a large team of brilliant and dedicated professionals. This story will end with me, for I have no belongings in the worldly sense. I have acquired nothing, built nothing, possess nothing—no family, sons, daughters.

> I am a well in this great land
> Looking at its millions of boys and girls
> To draw from me
> The inexhaustible divinity

And spread His grace everywhere
As does the water drawn from a well.

I do not wish to set myself up as an example to others, but I believe that a few readers may draw inspiration and come to experience that ultimate satisfaction which can only be found in the life of the spirit. God's providence is your inheritance. The bloodline of my great-grandfather Avul, my grandfather Pakir, and my father Jainulabdeen may end with Abdul Kalam, but His grace will never cease, for it is eternal.

SECTION 2

Inspirations

*An ignited mind is the
most powerful resource
on the earth,
above the earth and
under the earth.*

The Message in the Cave

In 2007, after the completion of my State visit to Greece as the President of India, I went to the Acropolis in Athens and saw the glorious ruins of a more than 5,000-year-old civilization. Then I trekked to the nearby Philopappos Hill to see the cave where Socrates, the great soul, was imprisoned and to the place of his self-sacrifice. The cave was dark and hiding inside was glorious history.

The surprise of a lifetime was in store for me there. Sensing a strange serenity in the cave, I requested for a brief solitude and the accompanying officials respectfully obliged. In the thinly lit cave I stood at the place where, declining the request of his friends to escape, Socrates drank the cup of poison as the punishment given to him for propogating inappropriate thoughts amongst the youth, and thus sacrificed his life.

My mind was filled with many questions. I went into a spell of reflection. Suddenly, I saw in my imagination a powerful streak of lightning and out of the dark corners of the cave came four images walking towards me in white robes. Foremost among them was Socrates who said in a soft voice, 'Thinking is freedom.' Next came Abraham Lincoln who said, 'No human being can be a slave of another.' Then I saw Mahatma Gandhi who said, 'O citizens of planet Earth, eliminate violence in all human missions, let peace prevail.' Finally, I saw the soul of science, Galileo Galilee who said, 'Truth is beyond human laws.' In front of all the four great minds, I stood humbled, speechless but inspired. The four great souls engulfed me in a fatherly embrace.

Socrates said, 'Kalam, 2,500 years have gone by, you are the only living leader who cared to visit my cave prison. Today is indeed a great divine event. We four sacrificed our lives for the cause of glory of human freedom and majesty of righteous life. All four of us know that you are concerned for the future of humanity and you are seeking wisdom for the twenty-first century planet Earth. We will not disappoint you.'

Each of the four figures then spoke thus:

Socrates said, 'For the growth of humanity and freedom of thinking, new patterns of thought should not be conditioned, confined or curbed. Thinking has to be the universal phenomenon.'

Abraham Lincoln said, 'Planet earth is paying the price for inequality amongst people. Slavery continues in its myriad forms. It is time that nations work for a sustained development, including more than half the citizens of the world who are poor and marginalized.'

Galileo said, 'My telescope revealed the truth that the earth orbits around the sun and many other cosmic truths. Scientific discoveries have empowered human lives. Science is the truest religion mankind has.'

Mahatma Gandhi proclaimed, 'Ahimsa Dharma, non-violence, is a very important positive force for peace on our plant. It will overpower every evil force that would arise to torment humanity.'

When I returned from the cave of Socrates, I realized I have a message to convey to the people emanating from the four great souls who lived on this earth in different space-times and enlightened the world with their knowledge, sacrificing their lives.

Humanity needs a great vision to forego all the conflicts and move towards a common goal of peace and prosperity for every human being. We foresee the birth of a world vision leading to a 'livable planet Earth'. This vision will be greater than any other goal ever aspired for by humanity.

Five Mighty Souls

OTHER THAN my parents and teachers, there are five persons, all of them scientists, who inspired and influenced me and whom I call the 'Mighty Souls'.

PROF. VIKRAM SARABHAI

I was fortunate to work with Prof. Vikram Sarabhai for seven years. While working closely with him, I saw the dawn of the vision for India's space programme. It was a one-page statement made in the year 1970 which stated, 'India with her mighty scientific knowledge and powerhouse of young should build her own communication, remote-sensing and meteorological spacecraft and launch from her own soil to enrich the Indian life in satellite communication, remote-sensing and meteorology.' Witnessing the evolution of this one-page vision into reality through many years of ceaseless work by a cosmic ray physicist and a great scientific mind was a great source of learning for me.

When I look at this one-page vision statement now and see the results it has created, I am overwhelmed. Today, we can build any type of satellite launch vehicle, any type of spacecraft and launch it from Indian soil, for which India has all the capability with its mighty facilities and powerful human resources.

PROF. SATISH DHAWAN

I learnt a great deal from Prof. Satish Dhawan, a great teacher at the Indian Institute of Science (IISc.), Bangalore and former Chairman of the Indian Space Research Organisation (ISRO). I worked with Prof. Satish Dhawan for a decade in the development of the first satellite launch vehicle programme for which I was fortunate to have been chosen project director.

Prof. Satish Dhawan gave to the country, especially to the young, a great leadership quality which we cannot find in any management book. He taught me a lot through his personal example. The most important lesson I learnt from him was that, when a mission is in progress there will always be some problems or failures, but the failures should not become the master of the programme. The leader has to subjugate the problem, defeat the problem and lead the team to success. This knowledge is embedded in me right from those days and has stood me in good stead throughout my life.

PROF. BRAHM PRAKASH

Another great teacher who inspired me was Prof. Brahm Prakash. When I was project director of SLV-3 programme, Prof. Brahm Prakash was the director of the Vikram Sarabhai Space Centre (VSSC).

As director, Prof. Brahm Prakash took hundreds of decisions for the growth of space science and technology. One important decision which I will always cherish was that once a programme such as SLV-3 was sanctioned, the multiple laboratories and centres of different organisations such as VSSC and ISRO, including the Space Department have to work together as a team to realize the stated goals of the programme. During 1973 to 1980 there was a tremendous financial crunch and there were competing demands from many small projects. But he converged all scientific and technological work to focus on the SLV-3 and its satellite.

Prof. Brahm Prakash is famous for the evolution of management with nobility and I would like to illustrate this with a few instances. He enabled for the first time the evolution of a comprehensive management plan for the SLV-3 programme towards the mission of putting the Rohini satellite in orbit. After my task team prepared the SLV-3 management plan, in a short period of three months, he arranged nearly fifteen brainstorming meetings of the Space Scientific Committee. After discussion and approval, this management plan was signed by Prof. Brahm Prakash and became the guiding spirit and the working document for the entire organization.

This was also the beginning of converting the national vision into mission mode programmes. During the evolution of the management plan, I could see how multiple views emerged and how people were afraid of losing their individuality due to the main mission, thereby causing much anger and resentment. In the midst of the various management meetings with smoke coming from the cigarettes continuously being lit one after the other, Prof. Brahm Prakash would radiate with a smile, and the anger, fear and prejudice all disappeared in his noble presence.

Today, the space programme, launch vehicle spacecraft, scientific experiments and launch missions all are taking place in the ISRO centres in a cohesive and cooperative manner. I thank this great mighty soul who was a very famous professor in metallurgy at the Indian Institute of Science and evolved the concept of management with nobility.

PROF. M.G.K. MENON

In a seemingly unconnected or maybe connected way some unique things happened in my life. And two great scientific minds were responsible for making them happen.

In 1962, I was working at the Aeronautical Development Establishment (ADE) in the Ministry of Defence as Senior Scientific Assistant. As the leader of the Hovercraft Development Programme I was responsible for designing, developing and piloting the hovercraft.

One day, my director told me that a great scientist was coming to ADE, and I must explain to him the design of the hovercraft and also give a flight demonstration. I saw in front of me a young bearded, philosopher-like personality. He was Prof. M.G.K. Menon, the then director of the Tata Institute of Fundamental Research. My God, how many questions he asked me in twenty minutes! I took him as a co-passenger in the hovercraft, and gave him a beautiful manoeuvred flight on the tarmac. He loved the flight and congratulated me. And I thought that that was the end of it, just like any other VIP visit.

But after a week, I received a telegram (there was no e-mail those days!) asking me to attend an interview for the post of Rocket Engineer at TIFR, Bombay. My ADE director helped me to get an airlift one way by taking special permission from the headquarters and I went for the interview. Three people were sitting at the interview board. What an interview! Prof. Sarabhai asked me questions on what I knew rather than what I didn't know; for me, this was a new way of interviewing. Within an hour, after the interview, I was told that I was selected and my life was steered from defence to the space programme.

DR RAJA RAMANNA

Another re-entry in my life took place after the completion of the SLV-3 mission. In the year 1981 a lecture series was organized at Mussoorie for a presentation of successful technological and scientific programmes of the nation. Before my presentation, Dr Raja Ramanna, the then scientific advisor to the Raksha Mantri gave a talk on Pokhran-I nuclear test and its technological and management challenges. I was the second speaker and Dr Raja Ramanna himself presided.

The topic I dealt with was the evolution of management systems for developing India's first satellite launch vehicle. During lunch time, Dr Raja Ramanna informed me that he wanted me to meet him for ten minutes. I still remember it was at 5 o'clock in the evening, on a Sunday in March 1981. The great nuclear scientist Dr Raja Ramanna told me that he was convinced that I could provide leadership to the missile programme envisaged by the Defence Research and Design Organization. The focal laboratory for the programme was the Defence Research and Design Laboratory (DRDL) and he invited me to become its director. I was delighted. That was the beginning of the story of my re-entry into defence leading to the evolution of the missile programme, and the rest is history. This 'mighty soul' was chairman of the Council of the IISc Bangalore, and was responsible for guiding its destiny for over ten years.

Like all re-entry problems, my re-entry into defence was also a tough job. Even though I was selected by Dr Raja Ramanna, Prof. Satish

Dhawan felt that I would not be able to succeed in the environment where I was to work. One person who came to my rescue was a close friend of Prof. Satish Dhawan and the then director of IISc, Prof. Ramaseshan. I got acquainted with him because of my interest in composite material development. It was Prof. Ramaseshan who persuaded Prof. Dhawan to allow my re-entry into the Defence Research and Development Organisation (DRDO), without which it would not have taken place.

The Joy of Reading

GOOD BOOKS become lifelong companions. They enrich our lives and guide us with their undying appeal and ability to talk to multiple generations of readers. One such book in my life is *Light from Many Lamps*. I bought it in the year 1953 from an old book store in Moore Market, Chennai. This book has been my close friend and companion for more than five decades. I have read and reread it several times and it has been re-bound many times. Whenever there is a problem, I turn the pages of the book and it soothes me and even points me to a path where a solution may lie. When happiness overwhelms me, the book again softly touches the mind and brings about a balanced thinking. Recently, a friend gifted me with a new edition of the book and I told him it was the best gift anyone could have given me. Fifty years from now, I am sure the book will still be available, perhaps in a new avatar. Truly, good books are eternal.

Another book that I have cherished is *Man the Unknown* by Dr Alexis Carrel, a doctor-turned-philosopher and a Nobel Laureate. This book highlights how the mind and body both need to be treated to cure an ailment as the two are integrated. You cannot treat one and ignore the other. I think this is an invaluable book for those who want to understand the connections of body and spirit, specially those who wish to become doctors. They will learn that the human body is not a mechanical system; it is a very intelligent organism made of psychological and physiological systems with a most intricate and sensitive feedback system.

Another book that has been my code of conduct for life is Thiruvalluvar's *Thirukkural*, a Tamil epic. I would like to recall one couplet from the *Thirukkural* which has influenced my life for the last six decades.

It says that whatever may be the depth of the river or lake or pond, whatever may be the condition of the water, the lily flower always blossoms. Similarly, if there is a determination to achieve a goal, even if it is impossible to achieve, the person will succeed.

There is another book that has enriched my thinking immensely. It is the autobiography of a village boy who went on to become the world's leading expert in laser technology. His name is Mani Bhaumik.

In 1968, an Indian scientist hailing from West Bengal, who was a PhD in Physics from IIT Kharagpur, was invited to join the team at the Research and Technology Center of Northrop Corporation, a major aerospace contractor who offered extraordinary facilities for a working physicist. He was working in the area of carbon monoxide (CO) laser. Based on his research, in 1968, his colleagues at Northrop demonstrated the most powerful continuous laser to date. In a further step forward, the Indian scientist was able to make the laser operate at room temperatures, something previously thought impossible.

The scientist, Dr Mani Bhaumik, presented his results at a University of California Los Angeles seminar. Edward Teller, the man whose revelatory insights had earned him the title 'Father of the H-Bomb' was there. Dr Teller was so intrigued by the presentation that when he felt nature's call and had to leave the room, he requested Dr Bhaumik to suspend the talk till he returned. A Soviet scientist later wrote in a prestigious Russian journal, 'After Bhaumik's thorough work on the CO laser, there isn't much left to do (on that laser).' His invention in laser led to the development of LASIK—an important application of eye surgery.

Dr Mani Bhaumik wrote a book called *Code Name God* integrating science and spirituality. I read the book in one sitting and enjoyed every chapter which brings out the pain and pleasure of the life of the author.

Stories of perseverance and extraordinary courage always inspire me. This piece in a book called *Everyday Greatness* by Stephen R. Covey has remained with me ever since.

Lindy and Geri had two daughters: Trudi, thirteen; and Jennifer, nine; and a son, Steven. At the age of eighteen months, Geri detected something abnormal with their son Steven. A CT scan by a neurologist revealed that the vermis, an area of the brain that transmits messages to and from the body's muscles, had not developed. The neurologist declared that Steven would never walk or talk and that his physical and mental functions would be severely affected. Geri couldn't eat or sleep for days. However, Trudi challenged the doctor's prognosis and announced that she did not believe what the doctor had said about Steven. She decided to work with her mother till Steven became normal. They started reading a passage to him every day at the dinner table, which became a habit. Jennifer and Trudi also asked questions and pointed out animals or people illustrated in books. For many weeks there was no response from Steven.

After three months, one evening, Steven suddenly wriggled away from the cushions. The family watched him inching towards the children's books. Steven flipped through the book till he saw the page filled with pictures of animals. Then, just as quickly as it opened, Steven's world shut down again. The following night, as Jennifer prepared to read, her brother crawled to the same book and opened the same page again. This showed that Steven's memory was continuously improving.

Both Trudi and Jennifer played the piano in the presence of Steven. One day, after practicing, Jennifer lifted Steven from his place under the piano. This time, he was uttering a new sound—he was humming the music and enjoying it. Simultaneously, the family also worked to build up his muscles. Geri, Trudi and Jennifer dabbed peanut butter on the boy's lips and, by licking it off, he exercised his tongue and jaw. When Steven was four and a half years old, he still couldn't speak words, but he could make some sounds and he had a remarkable memory. After studying a 300-piece jigsaw puzzle, he could assemble the pieces in one sitting.

After many rejections, Steven was admitted to the Robert Allen Montessori School run by Louise Bogart who found that Steven was determined to make himself understood.

One day, Bogart stood off to the side and was watching the teacher work with another child on numbers. 'What number comes next?' the teacher asked. The child drew a blank. Instead, the answer came from elsewhere. 'Twenty!' Steven blurted. Steven had not only spoken clearly, but had also given the correct answer. Bogart approached the teacher. 'Did Steven ever work on this?' she asked. 'No,' the teacher answered. 'We worked with him a lot on numbers one through ten. But we didn't know he had learned any beyond ten.' That day, Bogart told Steven's mother, 'This is just the beginning of what the Steven is capable of.' His motor skills remained poor, so Jennifer, Geri and Trudi continued to work hard with Steven, particularly on his motor skills. 'I can do it,' Steven assured Jennifer one day. 'Just give me time.'

After that, Steven continuously improved and was admitted to a mainstream Catholic school in 1990. Such is the power of collective determination to cure a child.

Books can be sources of inspiration for anyone, anywhere. In 2011, I went to Madurai to inaugurate the Paediatric Oncology unit of the Meenakshi Mission Hospital. After the programme, a person who looked very familiar approached me. When he came closer, I realized that he has been my driver when I was working with DRDL in Hyderabad. His name is V. Kathiresan, and he worked with me day and night for nine years. During that time, I had noticed that he was always reading in his spare time, be it a book, magazine or a newspaper. That dedication attracted me. One day, I asked him what made him read so much during his leisure time. He replied that he had a son and daughter and both asked him lots of questions. In order to give them correct answers, he read and studied whenever he got the time. The spirit of learning in him impressed me and I told him to study formally through a distance education course. I also gave him some free time to attend the course and complete his +2 and then to apply for higher education. He took that as a challenge and kept on studying. He did B.A. (History), then M.A. (History) and then he did M.A. (Political Science). He also completed his B.Ed and then M.Ed. Then he registered for his Ph.D in Manonmaniam Sundaranar University and got his Ph.D in 2001. He joined the education department of Tamil Nadu government and served for a number of years. In 2011, when I met him, he was an assistant professor in the Government Arts College at Mellur near Madurai. What extraordinary commitment and dedication had helped him to acquire the right skills in his leisure time and changed the course of his life.

It certainly doesn't matter who you are if you have a vision and determination to achieve that vision through the constant acquisition of knowledge.

When you wish upon a star,
Makes no difference who you are
Anything your heart desires
Will come to you.

In this context, I must emphasize the importance of home libraries. On 11 August 2009, I was participating in the valedictory function of the book fair festival at Erode in Tamil Nadu. While addressing the audience, I suggested that every one of the children present there allocate at least one hour a day for reading quality books. This will enrich them with knowledge and see them grow as great children. I also suggested all the parents should start a small library in their own houses with approximately twenty books to begin with, of which around ten should be children's books. This would help the children in the house to cultivate reading habits at an early age. Many people who attended this function appreciated this thought and decided to start a library at their homes. I told them to take this oath:

Today onwards, I will start a home library with twenty books, and out of which ten books will be children's books.
My daughter and son will enlarge this home library with 200 books.
My grandchildren will build a great home library of 2,000 books.
I consider our library a lifelong treasure and the precious property of our family.
We will spend at least one hour at the library to study along with our family members.

After taking this oath, a surprising event happened. Thousands of people rushed to the book stalls and within an hour most of the books at the book fair were exhausted.

A home library is the greatest wealth. Reading for one hour each day can transform our children into great teachers, leaders, intellectuals, engineers, scientists and, most importantly, into thinking adults. Apart from enriching the knowledge of every family member, a reading habit also creates healthy discussion among family members which is essential for the sustained harmony of the entire family.

The Presidential Years

*The twenty-first
century is about the
management of all the
knowledge and
information we have
generated and the value
addition that we can
bring to it.*

The Interactive President

Empowerment comes from within
Nobody else can give it, except the Almighty.

THE PRESIDENCY was a challenge for me. It became a platform to launch India 2020, which I believe can only be achieved by the participation of all citizens including elected representatives all the way up to Parliament, administrators, artists and writers, and the youth of the country. The best way to convince others of the relevance of this mission is through face-to-face discussion, which will also help in the assimilation of others' views and thinking.

The presidency provided me with this opportunity. I could communicate directly with people across the social spectrum, particularly the youth and the political leaders, regarding the importance of having a vision for the nation that should be translated into action.

This gave my role as President an additional purpose. In respect of the constitutional role, the President has to ensure that every action of the government and the legislatures is in line with the spirit of the Indian Constitution. Every action that the government takes is in the name of the President of India. The Bills and ordinances passed by Parliament and the government come to the President for assent and he has to ensure that these instruments are for the larger benefit of society. He also has to see that they do not set a precedent for taking an action that is biased. I will not dwell at length on the established principles and practices of the institution of President. However, besides those set by the Constitution, tradition and precedent, I felt that the role offers much more than merely that of the titular head of government.

There is scope for action on many fronts, whether it is on the

77

development front as a catalyst for achievement by communicating with different sections of the society; politically, as he has to personally assess the strength of the party or alliance in power, so that they do not take decisions when they do not have adequate numbers; providing sagacious advice to governors and learning about the functioning of their states; and as supreme commander of the armed forces inspire them to exemplary performance.

In addition, as head of state he is the focus of people's attention. My purpose was to make Rashtrapati Bhavan much more accessible to the people and use it for reaching out to them. It was my way of making them feel a part of the growth and prosperity of the nation and give them a stake in its governance. Thus, from being President I went to being part of people's lives, and the institution became a much more interactive one.

One of the first things I did at Rashtrapati Bhavan was to initiate e-governance. There were computers in use but I felt that the process needed to be taken much further. We implemented a system whereby all the files, documents, and letters which arrived at the President's Secretariat would first get digitized and bar coded. The paper files would then be archived. From then on the file moved only electronically to various officers, directors, secretaries to the government, and to the President, according to the importance of the file.

My dream was to have a system whereby Rashtrapati Bhavan was connected to the Prime Minister's Office, governors' offices and ministries over a secured messaging network with digital signatures thus enabling G2G e-governance operations. We had tested the system and it was ready for implementation. One day I hope my dream comes true. When we implemented e-governance across nine sections of the President's Secretariat, we checked if it had helped effectiveness. Normally, when the petitions from the citizens reached the Public-1 Section, for twenty petitions to get a decision, it used to take seven days, but after the implementation of e-governance it took only five hours to clear forty petitions. I hope one can see such systems in many more state and central government offices.

~

One of the important events in the early days of my presidency was inviting members of Parliament from the states and union territories for a series of breakfast meetings to the Rashtrapati Bhavan so that I could get first-hand knowledge about the status of development there. These meetings were held during a period of about three months in 2003—from 11 March to 6 May. They made a lasting impression on my mind.

The objective of each of these meetings was well laid out and my team and I spent several weeks preparing for them. We conducted research on the competencies and development requirements of each state. The required information was collected from the Planning Commission, government departments—both central and state— national and international assessments of the state and other relevant documents.

The data was analysed and put in a presentable form using graphics and multimedia. At the meetings, PowerPoint presentations were made to the MPs with an emphasis on three areas: 1) the vision for a developed India; 2) the heritage of the particular states or union territory; and 3) their core competencies. The objective was to stress the point that to achieve the development of the nation, it was vital to achieve the development of each of these areas. Hence a fourth aspect was also prepared—selected development indicators for each of them. And what an enrichment I got by way of preparation and by the contributions of the members of Parliament, who hailed from all parties. Meeting them helped me to understand the richness of the diverse parts of the country.

The first meeting was of parliamentarians from Bihar. I was encouraged by the enthusiasm of the members for the content of the presentation, which covered the national development profile in relation to that of Bihar, the state's core competencies and how to take the state to a developed status. The parliamentarians felt that the meeting was too short. While we increased the breakfast meeting time from sixty to ninety minutes, we had the pleasant experience that even after the meeting concluded, and after all the question-and-answer sessions, many members continued to show an interest in the presentation about their state. The meetings were put on record in a document as well.

Personally, I relished every moment of these meetings. They were a real education for me on the needs of each region. The preparations were complemented by field-level inputs from the MPs. Many of the members also told me that such comprehensive preparation was useful for them. As a matter of fact, these details and discussions continued to be a major communication bond between the MPs and myself throughout my presidency and beyond. Even now, when I meet them, development becomes a basis for conversation and discussion.

The evolution of India 2020 with inputs from many experts led me to focus on different aspects of societal transformation. The details of the states as discussed in the breakfast meetings gave me further assurance on the path to be followed for progress. The MPs gave me many useful ideas. I spoke at least nine times on the 2020 India vision in Parliament and addressed twelve state assemblies on the path to prosperity for a particular state. The type of questions and suggestions I received at the breakfast meetings paved the way to incorporate possible requirements for the state's development such as waterways, employment generation, activating public health centres, improving the connectivity of rural areas and enriching the education system in my database. This database, consisting of what I had presented to the MPs, became a reference tool to illustrate how India 2020 can be achieved when I addressed the national and state chambers of commerce and industry, management associations and technical institutions. Later, as a logical process, the ten pillars of development were evolved as a part of the vision. Today I address professionals, business leaders and researchers on how they can contribute with innovative ideas to achieve these ten pillars.

These are as follows:

1) A nation where the rural and urban divide has reduced to a thin line.

2) A nation where there is equitable distribution and adequate access

to energy and quality water.

3) A nation where agriculture, industry and the service sector work together in symphony.

4) A nation where education with value systems is not denied to any meritorious candidates because of societal or economic discrimination.

5) A nation which is the best destination for the most talented scholars, scientists and investors.

6) A nation where the best of healthcare is available to all.

7) A nation where the governance is responsive, transparent and corruption free.

8) A nation where poverty has been totally eradicated, illiteracy removed and crimes against women and children are absent and no one in the society feels alienated.

9) A nation that is prosperous, healthy, secure, peaceful and happy and follows a sustainable growth path.

10) A nation that is one of the best places to live in and is proud of its leadership.

The breakfast meetings also brought out how the leaders of the country could discuss development in a non-partisan manner. Rashtrapati Bhavan is indeed the only place where party differences disappear and the nation was seen as an integrated whole by every member of Parliament.

Apart from my meetings with MPs in Rashtrapati Bhavan, I had the opportunity to address the two Houses more than ten times.

The addresses are solemn occasions and I was heard in pindrop silence each time in the overflowing Central Hall. I had two types of interactions with Parliament. One was fully government-driven, for example the five budget speeches I gave, and the other was driven by my thoughts and ideas. Even in the government presentations, I would include certain thoughts that I wanted to discuss. Both Vajpeyeeji and Dr Manmohan Singh included my suggestions.

I used this forum to impress upon the parliamentarians their roles and responsibilities towards the nation. While addressing the parliamentarians in 2007 during a commemorative function to celebrate the 150th anniversary of our Independence movement, I conveyed a message that brings out the responsibilities of MPs to their respective constituencies, to their state and to the nation. I said: 'Our movement to true freedom and independence is still incomplete; our story is still unfolding... The time has now arrived for Parliament and legislative assemblies to emerge with a new vision and leadership to make our nation not only enlightened, united, harmonious, rich and prosperous, but above all, a safe nation, invulnerable forever to invasion and infiltration across its borders...

'The national leadership has to radiate confidence in our people and boldly emerge by formulating and implementing new national missions, targeting specific time-bound goals. India can be rightly proud of its many achievements in the economic, social and political fields over the past sixty years. But we cannot afford to rest content with past achievements and ignore recent developments that call for a change in technology, industry and agriculture. Many challenges need to be responded to: the emergence of multiparty coalitions as a regular form of government that need to rapidly evolve as a stable, two-party system; the need to strengthen internal security to cope with global terrorism and new forms of internal law-and-order problems; the widening of economic disparities during a period of high growth in the absence of a comprehensive National Prosperity Index in place of GDP alone; the rapid depletion of global fossil fuel reserves to be tackled by an energy independence programme; and increasing threats to our territorial security by the development of new forms of warfare...'

I also said: 'When I see you, honourable members of Parliament, particularly young members, I see in you the eternal spirit of Mahatma Gandhi, Dr Rajendra Prasad, Pandit Jawaharlal Nehru, Sardar Patel, Subhas Chandra Bose, Dr Ambedkar, Abul Kalam Azad, Rajaji and many great visionary leaders of our nation. Can you also become visionary leaders, putting the nation above yourself? Can you become one of the great ones of India? Yes, you can. You can, if you enliven the Parliament with leadership for the great mission of transforming India into an economically prosperous, happy, strong and safe nation before 2020. For that to happen, honourable members, you have to have a big aim and work for the nation in the Parliament and outside. History will remember you for launching a great, bold and swift mission for the nation, a notable departure from small and fragmented actions.'

~

While I was constantly engaged in working with elected members of the state assemblies and Parliament towards realizing the vision of India 2020, it was also important for me to utilize the office of governor—another important constitutional post—to work towards the same goal. In this respect, the governors' conferences held in Rashtrapati Bhavan during 2003 and 2005 become very important.

The 2003 conference was conducted against the backdrop of Prime Minister Vajpayeeji's commitment to ensure that India became a developed nation by 2020, as outlined in his Red Fort address the previous year and in Parliament. At the 2005 governors' conference, Prime Minister Manmohan Singh confirmed his government's commitment to the task of leading India to the same objective.

The impressive speeches at conferences get forgotten. However, I placed great value on what was said, and continue to remember it as showing a serious commitment to faster development. Vajpayeeji stated that every part of the administrative system must recognize the need for development and further this cause, which would enable an earlier realization of our goals. This was something I could appreciate, having seen the difficulties that arise in motivating different departments to work for a combined purpose. The participating governors took the opportunity to speak their minds in an uninhibited fashion. Overall, an environment was created in which every participant could discuss problems and their solutions.

During the 2005 conference, Dr Manmohan Singh was accompanied by all his Cabinet members for a detailed discussion on the issues of education, terrorism, disaster management and implementation of Value Added Taxation based on the agenda structured by the President's Office. Appreciating the contribution made by the governors in many areas of management development, the prime minister gave his assurance that he and his colleagues would also make every effort, guided by the inspiration provided by the president. I mention this to show how the President's Office became a very effective platform for my pet project.

~

The court cases pending in trial courts, high courts and the Supreme Court run into astonishing numbers in India. Even allowing for new cases that keep being filed, the count runs into the millions. For those involved in litigation, there is a huge cost in time, money and suffering.

In 2005, I had an opportunity to address the All India Seminar on Judicial Reforms with Special Reference to Arrears of Court Cases, where I talked about the evolution of a National Litigation Pendency Clearance Mission. I analysed the causes of delay in delivering justice, which are: 1) an inadequate number of courts; 2) an inadequate number of judicial officers; 3) the judicial officers are not fully equipped to tackle cases involving specialized knowledge; 4) the dilatory tactics followed by the litigants and their lawyers who seek frequent adjournments and delays in filing documents; and 5) the role of the administrative staff of the court.

Based on my analysis, I suggested encouraging dispute resolution through the human touch; reinforcing the Lok Adalats; creating a National Litigation Pendency Clearance Mission; ensuring alternative dispute redressal mechanisms such as arbitration; and providing fast-track courts.

I also suggested several actions with particular reference to pendency in the high courts. These included the classification of cases on the basis of an age analysis, that is, identifying cases that are redundant because the subsequent generations are not interested in pursuing them.

Primary among my recommendations was the e-judiciary initiative. As part of this, I recommended computerization of the active case files, taking into account the age analysis, which will surely reduce the number of cases that are still pending. We needed a database that would track a case from the time it was registered till it was settled with a judgement. This electronic tracking would enable easy search, retrieval, grouping, information processing, judicial record processing and disposal of cases in a transparent manner, and make the process quicker. The complainant can find out at any time at what stage the case is, in what court a hearing will be held and when, and which issues will be dealt with by the court, enabling him to be fully prepared for the case. Apart from bringing in total transparency, the judges would also be able to track the progress of the case, the number of adjournments that had been sought, whether the grounds for these were trivial or serious and other such information that would help in the delivery of justice.

Additionally, video-conferencing could be used in a big way. This would save an enormous amount of expenditure and the unnecessary movement of police personnel accompanying those under trial.

Video-conferencing is also very useful in cases where a number of individuals are accused. The witness identification and crime reconstruction areas have also immensely benefited from the use of ICT (Information and Communication Technology).

Many countries, for example Singapore and Australia, have also been experimenting with Internet courts and a legal consultation service that can advise potential litigants about the legal correctness of the case that he or she wishes to pursue. In all cases, the ICT had been useful in speedy redressal of the cases as well as in avoiding fraudulent cases. This in effect would contribute to speeding up our justice delivery system.

Finally, I gave the following nine suggestions which will enable our judicial system to administer timely justice to our citizens.

1) Judges and members of the bar should consider how to limit the number of adjournments being sought.
2) E-judiciary must be implemented in our courts.
3) Cases should be classified and grouped according to their facts and relevant laws.
4) Experts in specialized branches of law such as military law, service matters, taxation and cyber law should be appointed as judges.

5) The quality of legal education in all our universities should be improved on the pattern of law schools.

6) An exemplary penalty should be imposed on those seeking undue adjournments and initiating frivolous litigation.

7) Judges of high courts and district courts may follow the suggested model for the Supreme Court and enhance the number of cases decided by them by voluntarily working extra hours on working days and Saturdays.

8) 'Multi sessions in courts' should be instituted, with staggered timings, to enhance capacity utilization with additional manpower and an empowered management structure.

9) A National Litigation Pendency Clearance Mission should be created for a two-year operation for time-bound clearance of pending cases.

Over a period of time, I have found that our judiciary has taken note of these suggestions and has started their implementation in phases. For example, I was happy to hear of the settlement of a long-pending divorce case through video-conferencing; the husband was in India and the wife was in the United States.

~

India possesses one of the finest armed forces in the world; loyal, courageous and disciplined. The President is the supreme commander of the armed forces. In that capacity, I was always keen to know the environment in which our servicemen operated, their state of readiness, their problems and challenges. As a part of this mission, I visited a number of units of the army, navy and air force. My interactions with the officers and jawans also led me to visit units stationed in difficult terrains. Hence, I specially chose to go to Kumar post on the Siachen glacier, the world's highest battleground, where our troops operate in extreme cold. I also visited the submarine operations off the coast of Visakhapatnam, and flew in a Sukhoi-30 MKJ at nearly twice the speed of sound. I found these exciting experiences, and would like to share them with you.

~

I landed at Kumar post on Siachen glacier on 2 April 2004. The post is located at an altitude of 7,000 metres. It was snowing and the temperature was minus 35 degrees Celsius with heavy winds. When I reached the field station, three soldiers—Naik from Karnataka, Williams from West Bengal and Salim from Uttar Pradesh—shook hands with me. The warmth of their handshakes dispelled the chill of the place. It gave me the confidence that our nation is safe in the hands of the soldiers defending it in this difficult environment. Extraordinary leadership qualities are required to generate such confidence among troops in such difficult conditions.

~

On 13 February 2006, I experienced a journey underwater in a naval submarine. The submarine dove to a depth of about 30 metres and started cruising. I visited the control room, where the crew explained the functioning of the submarine, showing me the manoeuvring operations and buoyancy-control mechanisms with great enthusiasm. It was a thrilling experience for me to cruise with the chief of naval staff, Admiral Arun Prakash, and the young sailors and officers. During the review, I was shown the underwater communication, target identification and launch systems. This was followed by the firing of a torpedo to simulate an attack to show the combat capability of our underwater force. The torpedo showed remarkable homing ability. I realized the complexities involved in underwater warfare.

I met the ninety officers and sailors in the vessel. Each was busy in his job. It is not an easy one but they feel proud of their challenging mission. I was given a delicious vegetarian lunch and shown a presentation on the navy's submarine plans for the next thirty years. After three hours underwater, we surfaced and returned to shore. It was in all ways a memorable journey.

~

On 8 June 2006, I flew a sortie in a Sukhoi-30 fighter aircraft. The previous night, Wing Commander Ajay Rathore gave me lessons on how to fly. He taught me how to pilot the aircraft as well as handle the weapons control system. It was something I had wanted to do since 1958, when I became an engineer. After we were strapped in, the Sukhoi took off and soared to a height of 7,500 metres—25,000 feet—flying at a speed of over 1,200 kilometres per hour. Wing Commander Rathore suggested a few turns and other manoeuvres. Flying a fighter aircraft can be an intensive experience and I experienced a gravitational force of about three Gs, of course with a G-suit strapped on to protect against a blackout. During the sortie I tried to understand the various systems that were developed by Indian scientists and integrated into this aircraft. I was very happy to see the indigenously built mission computers, radar warning receivers, display processors and other equipment. I was shown how to locate a target in the air and on the ground with the help of synthetic aperture radar. The flight lasted for over thirty-six minutes. I felt it was the fulfilment of a long-cherished dream.

I had opportunities too to interact with members of our paramilitary forces, central and state police personnel and internal security forces. Their dedication and valour left a deep imprint on my mind.

As President I had the opportunity to meet the entire cross-section of our society. I used this interaction to understand people, their aspirations and challenges. Equally important, I could also bring people together for a common national mission.

Vision 2020: On Leadership, Governance and Abiding Values

*What matters in this life more
than winning for ourselves,
is helping others win.*

The Knowledge Society

Wisdom is a weapon to ward off destruction;
It is an inner fortress which enemies cannot destroy.
—Thirukkural 421 (200 BC)

ANCIENT INDIA was an advanced knowledge society. Invasions and colonial rule destroyed its institutions and robbed it of its core competencies. Its people have been systematically degraded to lower levels of existence. By the time the British left, our youth had lowered their aims and were satisfied earning an ordinary livelihood. India is essentially a land of knowledge and it must rediscover itself in this aspect. Once this rediscovery is done, it will not require much struggle to achieve the quality of life, strength and sovereignty of a developed nation.

Knowledge has many forms and it is available at many places. It is acquired through education, information, intelligence and experience. It is available in academic institutions, with teachers, in libraries, in research papers, seminar proceedings and in various organizations and workplaces, with workers, managers, in drawings, in process sheets and on the shop floors. Knowledge, though closely linked to education, comes equally from learning skills such as those possessed by our artists, craftsmen, hakims, vaidyas, philosophers and saints, as also our housewives. Knowledge plays a very important role in their performance and output too. Our heritage and history, the rituals, epics and traditions that form part of our consciousness are also vast resources of knowledge as are our libraries and universities. There is an abundance of unorthodox, earthy wisdom in our villages. There are hidden treasures of knowledge in our environment, in the oceans,

91

bioreserves and deserts, in the plant and animal life. Every state in our country has a unique core competence for a knowledge society. Knowledge has always been the prime mover of prosperity and power. The acquisition of knowledge has therefore been the thrust area throughout the world. Additionally, in India, there has been a culture of sharing it, not only through the tradition of guru-shishya but also by its spread to neighbouring countries through travellers who came to Nalanda and other universities drawn by their reputation as centres of learning. India is endowed with natural and competitive advantages as also certain distinctive competencies. But these are scattered in isolated pockets and the awareness of these is inadequate. During the last century the world has changed from being an agricultural society, in which manual labour was the critical factor, to an industrial society where the management of technology, capital and labour provide the competitive advantage. In the twenty-first century, a new society is emerging where knowledge is the primary production resource instead of capital and labour. Efficient utilization of this existing knowledge base can create wealth for us in the form of better health, education and other indicators of progress. The ability to create and maintain the knowledge infrastructure, to enhance skills and increase productivity through the exploitation of advances in various fields will be the key factors in deciding the prosperity of this society. Whether a nation qualifies as a knowledge society is judged by how effectively it deals with knowledge creation and knowledge deployment.

The knowledge society has two very important components driven by societal transformation and wealth generation. The societal transformation is with respect to education, healthcare, agriculture and governance. These will lead to employment generation, high productivity and rural prosperity.

The task of wealth generation for the nation has to be woven around national competencies. The Technology Information, Forecasting and Assessment Council (TIFAC) task team has identified core areas that will spearhead our march towards becoming a knowledge society. The areas are: information technology, biotechnology, space technology, weather forecasting, disaster management, tele-medicine and tele-education, technologies utilizing traditional knowledge, service sector and infotainment which is the emerging area resulting from the convergence of information and entertainment. These core technologies, fortunately, can be interwoven by information technology, a sector that took off only due to the enterprising spirit of the young.

Thus there are multiple technologies and appropriate management structures that have to work together to generate a knowledge society. With India carving a niche for itself in IT, the country is uniquely placed to fully capitalize on the opportunity to quickly transform itself into a knowledge society. The methodology of wealth generation in these core areas and to be able to meet an export target set at $50 billion by the year 2008, especially through the IT sector, is a subject that is currently under discussion. Also being discussed is how best to simultaneously develop the capability to generate IT products worth $30 billion domestically to pump in for societal transformation. I am glad that the Planning Commission has taken a lead in generating a roadmap for transforming India into a knowledge society. I had the opportunity to be the chairman of the Steering Committee set up for this task.

Evolving suitable policy and administrative procedures, changes in regulatory methods, identification of partners and, most important, creation of young and dynamic leaders are the components that have to be put in place. In order to generate wealth, which is the second component for establishing a knowledge society, it is essential that, simultaneously, a citizen-centric approach to shaping business policy, user-driven technology generation and intensified industry-lab-academia linkages have also to be established.

Becoming a knowledge superpower by the year 2010 is a very important mission for the nation. While a knowledge society has a two-dimensional objective of societal transformation and wealth generation, a third dimension emerges if India is to transform itself into a knowledge superpower. This is knowledge protection and it entails a tremendous responsibility. It is very important that our communication network and information generators are protected from electronic attacks through surveillance and monitoring. There should be a focussed approach to intellectual property rights and related issues, and our ancient knowledge and culture, too, are part of our resource base and need to be protected as such.

In 1960, the agriculture sector employed, in part or in full, 74 per cent of the population. This came down to 62 per cent in 1992 and is expected to further fall to 50 per cent by 2010, though the demand for agricultural products will double by then. Higher productivity and better post-harvest management will have to compensate for manpower reduction in the farming and agricultural products sectors.

There was a function in Chennai organized by the Manipal Academy of Higher Education who felicitated me along with the father of the Green Revolution, C. Subramaniam, and eminent lawyer N.A. Palkhivala. After the function, I shared with the ninety-year-old Subramaniam his vision of a second Green Revolution. He told me about his dream of setting up a national agro foundation that would develop hybrid seeds. His foundation would adopt small and marginal farmers and provide them with laboratory facilities for soil testing and access to information on the weather and markets, so that they could earn more through enhanced yields and better prices for what they produced. He aimed at bringing a million farmers under the scheme. Visionaries don't age!

On another occasion, I was talking to the students of Dr Mahalingam College of Engineering and Technology at Pollachi, near Coimbatore. Dr N. Mahalingam, a great industrialist and academician, was sitting with me. He was telling me how the country can generate wealth through agro, chemical and textile industries. Amazed by his achievements in establishing industries and educational institutions, I asked him, 'Sir, what is your next mission?' As I said this, I realized that I was asking this question of a person who was about eighty years old!

Dr Mahalingam replied, 'I have analysed the Tamil scripts used in the last Sangam, which was 2,500 years ago. Now I would like to do research on the Tamil scripts used in the first Sangam which existed 5,000 years ago!' It was another reminder to me that visionaries don't age.

In the case of industry, in 1960, 11 per cent of the population was engaged in small-scale and large-scale industries. The trend continued with 11 per cent even in 1992. However, it has to increase to 25 per cent in 2010, bearing in mind the envisaged GDP growth and increased competition as trade restrictions are lifted under the WTO. The pattern of employment will take a new shape. Employment in the service or knowledge industry has increased from 15 per cent in 1960 to 27 per cent in 1992. And it will further increase to 50 per cent in view of infrastructure maintenance areas and IT sector and entertainment demands. This big change will demand more trained personnel. Our leaders in commerce and industry have to prepare themselves for the transformation.

The fact that there is net migration from the villages to cities shows the disparities in living standards between the two. Ideally, both rural and urban areas should be equally attractive with no net migration either way. Near zero net rural-urban migration is a mark of development. How can we achieve that happy balance? Rural development is the only solution. This means providing rural areas with the amenities that are currently available only in cities. This would generate employment on the same scale, and at the same level, as in the cities in the rural areas too. The other challenge would be to provide these benefits at a small fraction of the financial, social, cultural and ecological costs the cities have to bear.

It is the expectation that this combination of generating employment bearing in mind environmental factors will make rural areas as attractive as cities are, if not even more attractive. Then, rural development may be expected to prevent, if not actually reverse, rural-urban migration. Hence, PURA (Providing Urban Amenities in Rural Areas) aims at integrated physical, electronic knowledge and economic connectivity.

Experience in India has demonstrated that the true handicap suffered by rural areas is poor connectivity and little else. Linking together a loop of villages by a ring road and high-quality transport may rectify that lacuna. Villages thus linked would also provide a large enough market to support a variety of services, which they would not be able to do individually. The ring road and the transport service together can convert the linked villages immediately into a virtual town with a market of tens of thousands of people. Such an area, which would also possess state-of-the-art telecommunication connectivity, will have a high probability of attaining rapid growth by setting up a virtuous cycle—more connected people attracting more investment, and more investment attracting even more people and so on. Basically, this involves selecting a ring of villages; connecting the villages on the ring by establishing a high-quality transport and telecommunication system; encouraging reputed specialists to locate schools, hospitals and other social services around the ring; marketing this well-serviced space to attract industry and commerce; and Internet connectivity.

The model envisaged a habitat designed to improve the quality of life in rural places and made special suggestions to remove urban congestion. Naturally, our most intractable urban problem is that of congestion. Efficient supply of water and effective waste disposal in every locality are the paramount civic needs. There is a minimum size below which a habitat is not viable and not competitive with the existing congested city. At the same time, the existing congested city is not economical compared to a new town once a minimum size of expansion is crossed. As against a conventional city that is, say, rectangular in shape and measuring 10 kilometres by 6 kilometres, the model considers an annular ring-shaped town integrating minimum eight to ten villages of the same 60 square kilometre area, and the same access distance of 1 kilometre to transport arteries. It needs only one transportation route of a distance half that needed for the rectangular-shaped city, so frequency of transportation will be doubled, halving waiting times. It has zero number of junctions and needs only one route as against the eight needed for the rectangular plan, so people will no longer need to change from one line to another. That saves transport time. Further, as all traffic is concentrated on one single route, high-efficiency mass transportation systems become economical even for a comparatively small population. This cuts costs substantially and is more convenient for the people.

Rural development is an essential need for transforming India into a knowledge superpower and high bandwidth rural connectivity is the minimum requirement to take education and healthcare to the rural areas. Roadmaps for development of certain areas have been generated and we have to work on their realization.

There was an invitation by Mr Ratan Tata, chairman of the Tata group of companies, to visit Telco at Pune, particularly to witness the challenge of designing, developing and manufacturing, in the country, a fully Indian car, the Indica. The prospect of the visit excited me. I thought I would get an answer to some questions that I have been asked on many occasions.

In 1980, when our team in ISRO launched the satellite launch vehicle and put Rohini into low-earth orbit, it was a big event for the nation. On 4 January 2001, when I saw the first prototype fighter aircraft, the Light Combat Aircraft (LCA), designed and developed indigenously by the Aeronautical Development Agency (ADA), taking to the skies, India was again described as one of the few countries to have acquired capabilities in this sophisticated field. This is the result of intensified networking between R&D laboratories, industry, academic institutions, users and the government.

Ratan Tata told me during the visit about his vision of making India a global player in the automobile sector. To implement his vision, he decided to acquire car manufacturing units from many countries rather than set them up here at considerable expense in terms of money and time. He looked towards manufacturing five times the present levels so that they could graduate to being globally competitive. This is a beautiful idea. I would add that Indian industrial complexes should become consortia as a first step and then envision becoming multinational companies.

I and my team are invited by a number of scientific, industrial, academic and management institutions to share our experiences in the pursuit of some of the national tasks I have mentioned. One question that came up during my interaction with students in Mumbai rings in my mind even now.

'Dr Kalam, we are very happy to see that India can build and produce its own SLVs and satellites, its own strategic missiles as also nuclear weapons and power stations. Can you tell me when India will design and produce its own passenger car with an Indian engine?'

When I was going through the design, manufacture of component, sub-assembly, integration and testing plants at Telco and was told that the company is producing about 60,000 cars annually, I was reminded of this question. I was not only witnessing the answer to it but also the technological strength of our nation.

I had another opportunity to see a concept take shape when Wipro invited me to participate in a function to mark the commissioning of a mobile heart care clinic at Bangalore in October 2000. This was a collaborative effort of Wipro-GE, Care Foundation and Klenzaids. My friend Arun Tiwari and I provided the system concept for the project. It was a great experience for me. After the inauguration I visited the Wipro-GE Centre that builds specialized medical equipment using advanced technologies. As soon as I entered, a young man approached me and pinned a national flag on my shirt. I shook his hand and asked him, 'Young man, will you stay and work for this country?'

He replied, 'Dr Kalam, I am in the profession of working on medical gadgets that are used for diagnosis. I am committed to a profession in which one tries to remove pain. I am needed here.' I was delighted by his answer. The centre itself struck me as a positive collaboration between two nations in the field of healthcare.

After the programme, Azim Premji, who heads Wipro, accompanied me to the Defence Research and Development Organization (DRDO) guest house. On the way, he explained how he was trying to assist elementary schools in Karnataka so that more children could be brought into the classroom. As we were having tea at the guest house, I asked him, 'How has Wipro reached its high stature in the business world?'

Premji gave a remarkable answer. 'Dr Kalam, I can say there are three aspects that come to my mind. One: Sweat for generations and the hard work of teams. Two: In Wipro we work for the customer's delight. Three: A bit of luck. The third point will not be of any consequence if the first two aspects are not achieved. In Wipro, what we have tried to do is wealth generation with social concern.'

A common thread runs through the experience of these institutions.

It is that we can deliver high-technology systems in spite of control and denial regimes. The presence of a competitive environment, networking capabilities, wealth generation with social concern and, above all, ignited minds of the young: these are all very important ingredients for building a knowledge society.

Maharishi Patanjali said in the *Yogasutra*, 'When you are inspired by some great purpose, some extraordinary project, all your thoughts break their bounds: Your mind transcends limitations, your consciousness expands in every direction, and you find yourself in a new, great, and wonderful world. Dormant forces, faculties, and talents become alive, and you discover yourself to be a greater person by far than you ever dreamed yourself to be.'

That is something addressed to all of us. It is the people of a nation who make it great. By their effort, the people in turn become important citizens of their great country. Ignited minds are the most powerful resource on earth, and the one billion minds of our nation are indeed a great power waiting to be tapped.

Education Enhances the Dignity of Human Life

Be a lamp, a life boat and a ladder.
Help someone's soul heal.
Walk out of your house like a shepherd.

—Jalaluddin Rumi

I ONCE READ a poem, 'The Student's Prayer', by a Chilean biologist, Mautrana. Some of the lines were:

Show me so that I can stand
On your shoulders.
Reveal yourself so that I can be
Something different.

Don't impose on me what you know,
I want to explore the unknown
And be the source of my own discoveries.
Let the known be my liberation, not my slavery.

When I read these words, the thought struck me that the best teachers are actually facilitators of innovation; of new ideas; creators of lifelong habit of innovative thinking.

Teachers are the backbone of any country—pillars upon whom all aspirations of the country are placed, and the ones who can turn these dreams into realities. I have been a teacher, too, and I felt I had been entrusted with a great responsibility to mould and give wings to young thoughts.

What is education? It is a learning process designed so that it leads to creativity. The result of the education process is to foster creativity. This comes from the environment in schools and each teacher's capability to ignite the minds of students. The essence of this thought has been put succinctly in the following verse:

Learning gives creativity
Creativity leads to thinking,
Thinking provides knowledge
Knowledge makes you great

What is this innovation that I mentioned earlier? Let me illustrate by giving the examples of six young innovators from various schools of our country who I met at Rashtrapati Bhavan on 2 September 2004.

The students and their innovations were:

- A system to prevent the soiling of railway tracks by Madhav Pathak of Jabalpur, Madhya Pradesh;
- Herbal pesticide tablets to be used in the storage of foodgrains by Priyanka Guleria of Sionty village, Punjab;
- Low-calorie biscuits made from banana peels by Rucha Joshi of Nanded, Maharashtra;
- A toy laser with educational applications by Sudhanwa Hukkeri of Belgaum, Karnataka;
- A software program for embedding text through audio signals by Kyan Pardiwalla of Mumbai, Maharashtra;
- An optically controlled wheelchair by S. Harish Chandra of Chennai, Tamil Nadu.

All these students were able to showcase their innovations at an exhibition for young innovators from all over the world held in Tokyo, Japan. They were chosen by the Confederation of Indian Industries (CII) and the Department of Science and Technology after a rigorous national-level selection process. I was happy to hear that their exhibits had recorded some of the highest footfalls at the international exhibition.

This example shows that our teachers are capable and motivated enough to groom young minds to innovate and come up with practical solutions for problems that plague our country and that are relevant to society. The success of students in this area is a testimony to their teachers' great service too, and I call this aspect of a teacher's job, capacity building.

The capacities teachers need to build among students in order to equip them to become nation builders are:

- The capacity for research or inquiry;
- Capacity for creativity and innovation, particularly the creative transfer of knowledge;
- Capacity to use high technology;
- Capacity for entrepreneurial leadership;
- Capacity for moral leadership.

The aim of the teacher should be to build character and human values and enhance the learning capacity of children through technology. They need to build confidence in children so they can think fearlessly and creatively.

India has around five million teachers working in primary and secondary schools. A majority of them teach in schools located in the 600,000 villages spread all over the country. Hence, it is important to make their lives comfortable and the profession an attractive one. This could be possible by improving infrastructure. The economic prosperity of the village unit is an important factor and depends on the physical, electronic and knowledge connectivity that each village enjoys in relation to the world. It is not adequate to provide only school infrastructure in a village, but we have to provide an integrated learning environment for the student and a stable economic environment for the whole family, which allow them to stay in the village.

Today, it is a natural tendency for teachers to look for transfers to urban areas since they feel they can educate their children only in big towns or cities. They also feel that their own knowledge can be expanded only with the facilities available in urban areas. This situation needs immediate attention by the government, and we should embark on a massive programme of providing integrated connectivities to villages. This is a multi-ministerial mission, which has to be executed in partnership with the corporate sector and others.

The role of the teacher is like the proverbial 'ladder'—it is used by everyone to climb up in life, yet the ladder stays in its place. Such is the noble nature of our profession. Like in the game of Snakes and Ladders (Parama padam) the ladder can take a person to the world of snakes or misfortune, or it can elevate to a world of unlimited fortunes. The teacher's place in society, according to ancient belief, comes after that of the parents and before that of God—mata, pita, Guru, devam. Which other profession enjoys such recognition and is as crucial to the development of the human race as a whole?

One person we all recognize as a great teacher was Dr Sarvepalli Radhakrishnan. This is what he had once said about teachers and the work required of them: 'It is well known that all great arts centre round religious leaders: music, painting, sculpture, literature, all these centre round and get inspiration from the great religious leaders. Great teachers do teach us those things etc. and they ask us to abolish caste, get rid of untouchability but it takes a long time for us to practice those teachings. We still suffer from these disabilities.' Only great teachers, and particularly the primary and secondary teachers, can remove this disability from our society.

To me, personally, being a teacher has given immense satisfaction and joy.

I gave a series of ten lectures on technology and societal change to the post-graduate students of Anna University. The vice chancellor told me, after appointing me a distinguished professor, that I would have sixty students in my class. But such was the enthusiasm for learning among the students there that each lecture had at least 150-200 pupils! At one of these lectures, I had shared the following anecdote from my own engineering education days. This happened in the Madras Institute of Technology (MIT), Chennai, where I studied from 1954 to 1957.

I had been assigned a project to design a low-level attack aircraft together with five other students. I was given the responsibility of doing the system design and system integration. Also, I was responsible for the aerodynamic and structural design of the project. The others in my team took up the design of propulsion, control, guidance, avionics and instrumentation of the aircraft. Our design teacher, Prof. Srinivasan, the then director of MIT, was our guide. One day, he reviewed the project and declared my work to be gloomy and disappointing. He refused to listen to my reasons—that I had had difficulties in bringing together the database from multiple designers. I asked for a month's time to complete the task, since I had to get the inputs from my teammates without which I could not complete the system design. Prof. Srinivasan told me, 'Look, young man, today is Friday afternoon. I give you three days' time. By Monday morning, if I don't get the configuration design, your scholarship will be stopped.'

This was a big jolt for me. The scholarship was my lifeline, without which I could not continue with my studies. There was no other way but to finish the task. My team too realized that we all needed to work together seamlessly in order to achieve this. We didn't sleep that night, working on the drawing board, skipping dinner. On Saturday, I took just an hour's break. On Sunday morning, I was near completion when I felt a presence in my laboratory. It was Prof. Srinivasan, studying my progress. After looking at my work, he hugged me affectionately. He said these words of appreciation which I never forgot: 'I knew I was putting you under stress and asking you to meet a difficult deadline. You have done a great job in completing this system design.'

Through this review mechanism, Prof. Srinivasan injected the necessity of understanding the value of time for each team member and made us understand that engineering education is also about system design, system integration and system management.

I realized then that if something is at stake, the human mind gets ignited and its working capacity gets enhanced manifold. That's exactly what happened. This is one of the techniques of building talent. The message is that the young in the organization, whatever be their specialization, must be trained in such a way that they are prepared for new products, innovation and for undertaking higher organizational responsibilities.

The other important factor in a teacher's life is research. Good teaching emanates from time spent in research. A teacher's love for research and experience in research are vital for the growth of the institution. Any institution is judged by the level and extent of the research work it accomplishes. This sets in motion a regenerative cycle of excellence. Experience of research leads to quality teaching and quality teaching imparted to the young, in turn, enriches the research.

Technological innovation is what lends the edge to economic competitiveness. The application of science leads to the development of technology. New technology changes the economy and the environment as society will develop with the introduction of relevant and useful technology.

Ultimately, education in its real sense is the pursuit of truth. The teacher is in the pivotal position. Teachers have to continuously replenish and update their own knowledge so that the students can rely on them as the sources of knowledge, and even more importantly, of love and caring. The teacher must look for newer opportunities to teach the latest technological developments and even use them in classrooms so that technology-assisted learning becomes the order of the day in India.

Education is an endless journey. Such a journey opens up new vistas of development of humanism where one can strive to rise above pettiness, disharmony, jealousy, hatred or enmity. It transforms a human being into a wholesome unit, a noble soul and an asset to the universe. Real education enhances the dignity of a human being and increases his or her self-respect. If only the real sense of education could be realized by each individual with the guidance of the teacher, and carried forward in every field of human activity, the world would be a better place to live in.

To this end, I have designed an oath for teachers.

I will love teaching. Teaching will be my soul.

I realize that I am responsible for shaping not just students but ignited youths who are the most powerful resource. I will be fully committed for the great mission of teaching.

As a teacher, it will give me great happiness if I can transform an average student of the class to perform exceedingly well.

All my actions with my students will be with kindness and affection like a mother, sister, father or brother.

I will organize and conduct my life in such a way that my life itself is a message for my students.

I will encourage my students and children to ask questions and develop the spirit of enquiry, so that they blossom into creative enlightened citizens.

I will treat all students equally and will not support any differentiation on account of religion, community or language.

I will continuously build capacities in teaching so that I can impart quality education to my students.

I will celebrate the success of my students.

I realize by being a teacher, I am making an important contribution to all the national development initiatives.

I will constantly endeavour to fill my mind with great thoughts and spread nobility in thinking and action among my students

Creative Leadership: The Essence of Good Governance

Before you do anything, stop and recall the face of the poorest, most helpless, destitute person you have seen and ask yourself, 'Is what I am about to do going to help him?'

—Mahatma Gandhi

LEADERSHIP IS THE ESSENCE OF GOOD GOVERNANCE

What are the characteristics of good leadership?

- A leader should be ready to give to others rather than expect others to give to him;
- A leader should be equipped to manage change;
- A leader should have nobility of heart;
- A leader should have vision and clear thinking, and the capacity to be a facilitator.

How do we make the governance system of our country most effective in order to ensure the development of the nation and to sustain it as an economically developed, prosperous, happy and peaceful society? For that we need creative leadership in all segments of the governance of the nation.

I have seen three national programmes succeed with the help of creative and effective leadership despite several challenges: the space programme of ISRO (Indian Space Research Organization), the AGNI programme of DRDO (Defence Research and Development Organization) and PURA (Providing Urban Amenities in Rural Areas).

In all these areas, I have seen that a true leader needs to be passionate, with the ability to travel on uncharted territory and courage to take quick and effective decisions. A true leader also needs nobility and honesty of vision.

Let me illustrate these characteristics through our national programmes.

VISION FOR SELF-SUFFICIENCY IN FOOD

The vision for India's Green Revolution was formed in the 1970s under the leadership of C. Subramaniam. With his visionary leadership, and with the scientific leadership of Nobel Laureate Dr Norman Borlaugh and Dr M.S. Swaminathan, and the active support of B. Sivaraman, Secretary Agriculture, in partnership with agricultural scientists and farmers, the team liberated India from the situation of what was called a 'ship-to-mouth existence'. Through an effort of historical magnitude, India attained near self-sufficiency in food through the 'seed to grain' mission. Because of the Green Revolution, the country is now able to produce over 236 million tonnes of food grain per year. Of course, farmers played a pivotal role in working alongside agricultural scientists to make this possible.

Political and scientific leadership has been able to build capacity among our scientists, researchers and farmers and so we are now taking up the mission of the Second Green Revolution which involves knowledge graduation from the characterization of soil to the matching of the seed with the composition of the fertilizer, effective water management and evolving pre-harvesting techniques for such conditions. Under this project, the domain of a farmer's work would enlarge from merely production of grains to food processing and marketing.

The Second Green Revolution will enable India to further increase its productivity in the agricultural sector. By 2020, India envisions the production of over 340 million tonnes of food grain in view of population growth and increased purchasing power. The increase in production would surmount many impeding factors such as reduced availability of land, shortage of water and reduction in availability of agricultural workforce. Our agricultural scientists and technologists, in partnership with farmers, have to work towards increasing the average productivity per hectare by three times of the present productivity. New technology would also be needed in the development of seeds that would ensure high yield even under constraints of water and land.

PASSION TO REALIZE A VISION

Now let me give you an example of how the passion to realize a vision has facilitated the successful and on-time implementation of a two-billion-dollar metro-rail project by the managing director of a public sector organization.

The Delhi Metro Rail Project has opened up the potential of executing a fast transportation system throughout the country that uses high technology with reliability. Delhi, the capital of the country with over twenty million people, has the distinction of having a world-class metro rail with front-line technology.

The work on the metro rail commenced on 1 October 1998 and the first phase, with three lines covering 65 kilometres, was completed by December 2005. Today, the overall route length of the Delhi Metro is around 190 kilometres. Every day, the metro handles a minimum of two million passengers.

The Delhi Metro Rail Corporation has brought to the country the most advanced rail technologies available. The notable components of the Delhi Metro are: lightweight stainless steel; sleek, modern trains with pneumatic springs; regenerative braking; public information display; wide vestibules and automatic doors. The sophisticated coach technology, which was not available in the country so far, has been transferred to BEML (Bharat Earth Movers Ltd.), Bangalore, which is now in the process of assembling these trains with progressive indigenization. BEML is now in a position to meet the upcoming requirement of trains in other cities of the country.

E. Sreedharan, the then managing director of the Delhi Metro Rail Corporation, had ensured that all the scheduled sections were completed on or before the target date and within their respective budgets. This dedicated and transparent leadership, backed by professional competence, gave the nation one of the best transportation systems in the world at the most economical cost. E. Sreedharan has since been a recipient of many national and international awards. He has been in demand to undertake the development of metro systems in other countries, which he has politely declined due to his commitment to Indian programmes.

TRAVELLING THE UNEXPLORED PATH

I was fortunate to work with Prof. Vikram Sarabhai for seven years. While working closely with him, I saw the dawn of the vision for the space programme in a one-page statement. Witnessing the evolution of this page, and to be a part of the team that worked ceaselessly for many years to realize this vision, has been a great learning experience for me. The famous vision statement of Professor Vikram Sarabhai made in the year 1970 states, 'India, with her mighty scientific knowledge and power house of young, should build her own huge rocket systems (satellite launch vehicles) and also build her own communication, remote sensing and meteorological spacecraft and launch from her own soil to enrich Indian life in satellite communication, remote sensing and meteorology. The projects selected in the space programme are designed to meet the societal needs.'

If I look at the original vision statement today, I am overwhelmed to see the results of this statement. Today, there are a total of 150 transponders in the geo-synchronous orbit for providing connectivity to the nation. Today, India can build any type of satellite launch vehicle or any type of spacecraft and launch them from Indian soil. India has launched Chandrayaan and the Mars Orbiter Mission. India has proved that through space science and technology, we can provide effective communication, resource-mapping, disaster-prediction and disaster-management systems.

MANAGING SUCCESSES AND FAILURES

Leaders with great minds are always looking for the right people to steer a project. The right people are self-driven, self-motivated and have no need of constant monitoring. For innovation to flourish, we must respect zeal and sincerity, irrespective of age and experience.

Three decades ago, while I was working at ISRO, I had a learning experience that has stayed with me my entire life.

I was given a task by Prof. Satish Dhawan, then the chairman of ISRO, to develop the first satellite launch vehicle, SLV-3, to put the Rohini satellite into orbit. This was one of the largest high-technology space programmes undertaken in 1973. The whole space technology community, men and women, were geared up for the task. Thousands of scientists, engineers and technicians worked relentlessly towards the realization of the first SLV-3 launch on 10 August 1979.

SLV-3 took off in the early hours and the first stage worked beautifully. But even though all the stage rockets and systems worked, the mission could not achieve its objectives, as the control system malfunctioned in the second stage. Instead of being placed in orbit, the Rohini satellite went into the Bay of Bengal. The mission was a failure.

There was a press conference at Sriharikota after the event. Prof. Dhawan took me to the press conference. And there he announced that he took full responsibility for not achieving the mission, even though *I* was the project director and the mission director.

When we launched the SLV-3 again on 18 July 1980, we successfully placed the Rohini satellite into orbit. Again there was a press conference and this time, Professor Dhawan put me in front to share the success story with the press.

What we learn from this event is that a true leader gives credit for success to those who worked for it, and takes responsibility for the failures of his team. That is true leadership. The scientific community in India has been fortunate to work with such leaders.

This is an important lesson for all the young people who are aspiring to be tomorrow's leaders. The great lesson we learn here is that a leader in any field—political, administrative, scientific, education, industry, judiciary, or any other human activity—should have the capacity for creative leadership and the courage to take responsibility for failures and share successes with his team members.

COURAGE TO TAKE DECISIONS

I still remember an incident from May 1996. It was nine o'clock at night when I got a call from the then prime minister P.V. Narasimha Rao's house saying that I should meet him immediately. I met him just two days before the announcement of the general election results. He told me, 'Kalam, be ready with your team for the nuclear test. I am going to Tirupati. Wait for my authorization to go ahead with the test. The DRDO-DAE teams must be ready for action.'

Of course, the election results that year were quite different from what he had anticipated. I was busy at the Chandipur missile range. I got a call saying that I must meet immediately with the prime minister designate, Atal Bihari Vajpayee, along with Narasimha Rao. I witnessed a unique situation. Shri Narasimha Rao—the outgoing prime minister—asked me to brief Vajpayeeji about the details of the nuclear programme, so that a smooth takeover of such an important programme could take place. This incident reveals the maturity and professional excellence of a patriotic statesman who believed that the nation's cause was bigger than party politics. After taking over as prime minister in 1998, the first task Vajpayeeji gave me was to conduct the nuclear test at the earliest. Both these leaders had the courage to take difficult decisions boldly, even though the consequences of such a decision could have great national and international significance.

NOBILITY IN MANAGEMENT

The next leader I would like to discuss is Prof. Brahm Prakash. When I was the project director of the SLV-3 programme, Prof. Brahm Prakash was the director of the Vikram Sarabhai Space Centre (VSSC), which integrated multiple institutions based on the advice of Prof. Kamala Chowdhuri, a management guru from the Indian Institute of Management.

Prof. Brahm Prakash took hundreds of decisions for the growth of space science and technology. One important decision, which I will always remember, was that once a programme such as the SLV-3 was sanctioned, the multiple laboratories of the VSSC as well as the multiple centres of ISRO, including the Space Department, would work to realize the stated goals of the programme *as a team*. Particularly during 1973–1980, there was a tremendous financial crunch and there were competing requirements from many small projects. He effectively converged all scientific and technological work to be focused towards SLV-3 and its satellite.

When I say that Prof. Brahm Prakash is famous for the evolution of management with nobility, I would like to give a few instances. He enabled the evolution of a comprehensive management plan for the SLV-3 programme towards the mission of putting the Rohini satellite in orbit for the first time. After my task team prepared the SLV-3 management plan, he arranged nearly fifteen brainstorming meetings of the SSC (Space Scientific Committee) over a period of three months. After discussion and approval, this management plan was signed by him and it became the guiding spirit and the working document for the whole organization.

This was also when the national vision on space was getting converted into mission mode programmes. During the evolution of the management plan, I could see how multiple views had emerged and how many people were afraid of losing their individuality to the main mission, thereby leading to much debate and anger at the meetings. I remember how Prof. Brahm Prakash presided over these meetings, with a radiant smile on his face. The anger, fear and prejudice all eventually disappeared in his presence.

Today, the space programme, launch vehicle, spacecraft, scientific experiments and launch missions all take place in the centres of ISRO in a cohesive manner. I learnt the hard way from him that before starting any programme, it is essential to have a project management plan, with the details of how to steer the project through different phases and how to foresee possible critical paths and possible solutions, keeping time, performance and schedule as key factors.

WORKING WITH INTEGRITY AND SUCCEEDING WITH INTEGRITY

In November 2011, I was in Jorhat, Assam, to address the World Tea Science Congress. The evening I reached, I addressed the administrative and police officers of Jorhat and Dibrugarh district in a session organized by R.C. Jain, district magistrate, Jorhat. There I administered an oath to the participants: 'I will work with integrity and succeed with integrity.' The decibel level was very high when they said 'work with integrity' but it went down when they were repeating 'succeed with integrity'.

The next day, I was at the World Tea Science Congress in the presence of the chief minister of Assam and the Jorhat adminsitrative team. There I saw a beautiful sight. The chairman of the Tea Board, M.G.V.K. Bhanu, an IAS officer, who was giving the introductory speech to the participants of the Congress said, 'Yesterday, Dr Kalam administered an oath to all the IAS and IPS officers, including myself. I would to like to assure you, Dr Kalam, that I have worked with integrity and succeeded with integrity for the past twenty-four years as an IAS officer in different parts of the state and the centre. Now I am with the Tea Board. I have also served as secretary to the CM of Assam. I would like to assure Dr Kalam that I have tried to maintain moral uprightness in all my tasks.'

Mr Bhanu also mentioned that he had been thinking about what he should be remembered for and he wanted to make India the largest producer and exporter of tea in the world.

If every functionary of the government of India has such vision and mission, I am confident that we will transform into a developed nation well before 2020.

NATIONAL DEVELOPMENT AND CREATIVE LEADERSHIP

These are the connections between creative leadership and how it can bring about national development.

- A nation's economic development is powered by competitiveness.

- Competitiveness is powered by knowledge.
- Knowledge is powered by technology and innovation.
- Technology and innovation are powered by resource investment.
- Resource investment is powered by return on investment.
- Return on investment is powered by revenue.
- Revenue is powered by volume and repeat sales.
- Volume and repeat sales are powered by customer loyalty.
- Customer loyalty is powered by the quality and value of products.
- Quality and value of products is powered by employee productivity and innovation.
- Employee productivity is powered by employee loyalty.
- Employee loyalty is powered by employee satisfaction.
- Employee satisfaction is powered by the working environment.
- Working environment is powered by management innovation.
- Management innovation is powered by creative leadership.

For success in all national missions, it is essential to have creative leaders. Creative leadership involves exercising the vision to change the traditional role from the commander to the coach, manager to mentor, from director to delegator and from one who demands respect to one who facilitates self-respect. For enhancing enterprise value, we need a large number of creative leaders.

VISION FOR THE NATION AND GOVERNANCE

When India transforms into an economically developed nation, our citizens can live in a green clean environment without pollution, have prosperity and peace. I am sure that the qualities of creative leadership discussed here will lay the foundations for the transformation of India.

Abiding Values

RIGHTEOUSNESS

There is a beautiful song emanating that advocates global peace through the development of righteousness:

> Where there is righteousness in the heart,
> There is beauty in the character.
> When there is beauty in the character,
> There is harmony in the home.
> When there is harmony in the home,
> There is order in the nation.
> When there is order in the nation,
> There is peace in the world.

We can see a beautiful connectivity of heart, character, nation and the world. How to inject righteousness in the human heart? This, indeed, is the purpose of human creation.

We are going through a complex situation as many of us are at war with ourselves, with society and with the world. At every instant there is a war in our mind, whether we should go in one direction or another. Whenever there is a dilemma, we must seek wisdom from the Almighty to lead us to the path of righteousness.

In a society we have to build righteousness among all its constituents. For the society as a whole to be righteous we need creation of righteousness in family, righteousness in education, righteousness in service, righteousness in career, righteousness in business and industry, righteousness in civil administration, righteousness in politics, righteousness in government, righteousness in law and order, and righteousness in justice.

RIGHTEOUS HOMES

If a country is to be corruption free and become a nation of beautiful minds, the three key societal members who can make a difference are father, mother and teacher.

One of the staff members of the Indian Institute of Science at Bangalore shared with me this incident. He said that he had taught his daughter that she should always speak the truth and that if she were to do so she would have nothing to fear in life. Today she is ten years old but when she was in the second standard, once she had missed school for a day because she had gone with her father to a function at his friend's place. In her leave letter the father wrote that due to unavoidable circumstances his daughter couldn't attend school. She immediately remarked, 'Why should I say unavoidable circumstances and not that we had to attend a function? You have taught me not to tell lies. Why should I tell lies?' The father immediately realized his mistake and re-wrote the leave letter giving the true reason for his daughter's absence.

This is the power of teaching children at a young age to be honest, which also enables us to be corrected by the child if we deviate from our righteous path. Honesty comes out of righteousness. Once taught, the children become conscience keepers. Once you start giving the right direction to the minds of the children, character building emanates within the family. 'I will make my home a righteous home' should be the motto of each and every child and every parent.

During one of my interactions with students, a student from Shimoga in Karnataka asked me the following question: 'What role can students play to stop corruption which is so deeply rooted in our country like cancer?' The agony of the young mind is reflected in this question. For me it was an important question since it comes from a young mind. I said there are one billion people in the country and nearly 200 million homes. In general there are good citizens everywhere. However, if we find that people in a few million homes are not transparent and not amenable to the laws of the country, this is what we can do: These homes, apart from parents, have one daughter or one son or both. If the parents in these homes are deviating from the transparent path the children can use the tool of love and affection and correct the parents to come back to the right path.

I asked all the children assembled in the gathering that, in case parents of a few children deviate from transparency, would they boldly tell their parents that they are not doing the right thing? Most of the children spontaneously responded, 'We will do it.' This confidence comes because they have love as a tool.

Similarly, I have asked the parents the same question at several other meetings. Initially there is a silence, but later, many of them hesitantly agree that they would abide by the children's suggestion since it is driven by love. They also take an oath that 'I will lead an honest life, free from all corruption and will set an example for others to adopt a transparent way of life.'

MOTHER GIVES THE PRINCIPLE OF TRUTH

Sheikh Abdul Qadir Al-Gelani was a great saint who lived in Afghanistan about one thousand years ago. One day, when child Abdul Qadir was grazing his cows, he heard a cow saying, 'What are you doing here in the grazing fields? It is not for this that you have been created.' He promptly ran back to his house feeling utterly terrified and climbed on to the roof of his house. From there he saw a large group of people returning from the Arafat Mountain, after performing Haj. Bewildered, Abdul Qadir went to his mother and asked her permission to make a journey to Baghdad to pursue a career in knowledge. His mother heard the divine call and promptly gave permission to Abdul Qadir to go. She gave him forty gold coins, which was his share of inheritance from his father, and stitched them inside the lining of his coat. When she stepped out of the door to bid him farewell, she said, 'Oh, my son! You are going! I have detached myself from you for the sake of Allah knowing that I shall not see your face again until the day of the last judgment. But take one advice from your mother: Always feel the truth, speak the truth and propagate the truth even when your life is at stake.'

Abdul Qadir set out with a small caravan heading for Baghdad. While passing through rough terrain a group of robbers on horses suddenly attacked the caravan and started looting. None of them however took the slightest notice of Abdul Qadir, until one of the looters turned to him and said, 'You here! Poor beggar! Do you have anything with you?' Abdul Qadir replied, 'I have got forty dinars which are stitched by my mother in the lining of my coat underneath my armpit.' The looter smiled and thought that Abdul Qadir was just joking and left him alone and moved elsewhere. A second looter came and asked the same thing. Abdul Qadir again repeated his answer. This looter also didn't believe him and left him. When their leader came they took Abdul Qadir to their leader and said to him, 'This boy looks like a beggar but claims that he is in possession of forty gold coins. We have looted everybody but we have not touched him because we don't believe that he has got gold coins with him and is trying to fool us.' The leader put the same question to Abdul Qadir who gave the same reply. The leader ripped open his coat and discovered that indeed Abdul Qadir had forty gold coins inside the lining of his coat. The astonished leader asked Abdul Qadir what prompted him to make this confession. Abdul Qadir replied, 'My mother made me promise always to be truthful even at the cost of my life. Here, it was a matter of only forty dinars. I promised her and shall never betray her trust, so I told the truth.'

The looters started weeping and said, 'You have adhered to the advice of your great mother but we have been betraying the trust of our parents and the covenant of our Creator for many years. From now onwards, you shall become our leader in our repentance.' And they all decided to give up robbing and looting and become righteous persons. This is how the world saw the birth of a great saint, Sheikh Abdul Qadir Al-Gelani, starting from an advice a mother gave to her child.

IMPARTING MORAL VALUES

After every child is nurtured during the early years with love and affection, when he reaches school-going age he needs value-based education. The prime learning period for a child is from six to seventeen years of age. Hence, the school hours are the best time for learning, and children need the best environment and mission-oriented learning with a value-based educational system.

While I was studying at St. Joseph's College in Trichy, I remember the lectures given by Rev. Father Rector Kalathil. He would talk about great spiritual, religious and political leaders and the qualities that make for a good human being. I am convinced that what I learnt in that class of moral science stands by me even today.

It is essential that schools and colleges arrange a lecture by a great teacher of the institution once a week for one hour on India's civilizational heritage. This class can be called a moral science class. This will elevate the young minds to love the country, to love other human beings and elevate the young to higher planes.

The right kind of education on moral values will upgrade the society and the country.

GIFT EXTINGUISHES THE DIGNITY OF HUMAN LIFE

Rameswaram is a beautiful island and I lived there as a young boy with my family. It was around 1940, and the Second World War was in progress when the Rameswaram Panchayat Board elections took place and my father was elected as a member; and the very same day he was also elected as president of the Board. My father was elected as the president not because he belonged to a particular religion or a particular caste or because he spoke a particular language or for his economic status, but only on the basis of his being a good human being. I was a school boy at that time, studying in the fourth class, and I still remember an incident that took place the day my father was elected.

Those days we did not have electricity and I would study with the light of a kerosene lamp. I used to learn by reading out aloud and was reading my lessons loudly when I heard a knock at the door. People never locked their doors in Rameswaram at the time. Somebody opened the door and came in and asked for my father. I told him that father had gone for evening namaz. He said, 'I have brought something for him, can I keep it here?' Since my father was not home, I shouted for my mother to get her permission. But as she had also gone for namaz there was no response. So I asked the person to leave the items on the cot, and I went back to my lessons.

I was reading aloud and fully concentrating on my studies when my father came back and saw a tambalum kept on the cot. He asked me, 'What is this? Who has given it?' I told him somebody came and left it for him. He opened the cover of the tambalum and saw a costly dhoti, angawastram, some fruits and sweets and the slip of paper that the person had left behind. I was the youngest son of my father and he really loved me. But this was the first time I ever saw him get so angry and it was also the first time that I got a beating from him. I got frightened and started crying. My mother rushed and embraced me and started consoling me. Seeing me cry my father touched my shoulder lovingly with affection and advised me never to receive any gift without his permission and explained that receiving a gift with a purpose is a very dangerous thing in life. He quoted a verse from Hadith which means, 'Gifts accompany poisonous intentions.' This experience taught me a valuable lesson for life which is deeply embedded in my mind even today.

Writings in the *Manusmriti* warn all individuals against accepting gifts given with a motive since it places the acceptor under an obligation to the person who gives the gift. Ultimately it results in making a person do things which are not permitted by law in order to favour the person who has given the gift. Therefore it is necessary that the quality of not yielding to the attraction of gifts and presents must be inculcated in individuals, so that they may develop immunity against the desire for receiving gifts. It is also said that by accepting gifts the divine light in a person gets extinguished.

CULTIVATE YOUR CONSCIENCE

Conscience is the divine light of the soul that burns within the chambers of our psychological heart. It is as real as life is. It raises its voice in protest whenever anything is thought of or done which is contrary to righteousness.

Conscience is a form of truth that has been transferred through our genetic stock in the form of knowledge of our own acts and our feeling of right or wrong.

Conscience is also a great ledger where our offences are booked and registered. It is a terrible witness. It threatens, promises, rewards and punishes, keeping all under its control. If conscience stings once, it is an admonition; if twice, it is a condemnation.

Cowardice asks, 'Is it safe?'

Greed asks, 'Is there any gain in it?'

Vanity asks, 'Can I become great?'

Lust asks, 'Is there pleasure in it?'

But Conscience asks, 'Is it right?'

Why have we become deaf to the voice of our conscience? Insensitive to its pricks? Callous to its criticism? The answer is corruption.

Corruption is an assault on the conscience. The habit of taking bribes and seeking favours has become very common. People holding important positions have developed inconsiderateness towards their conscience. They pretend that everything is all right. Do they not know of the law of action and reaction? Have they forgotten how impressions of the subconscious mind and its forces work? If you take bribes, your thoughts and actions are registered in the subconscious mind. Will you not be carrying forward your dishonesty to the next generation and causing them great suffering?

It is a painful reality that corruption has become a way of life affecting all aspects of our life, personal as well as social. It is not merely pecuniary corruption but its other forms as well. Immoral ways of people holding high positions and handling power have taken the feeling of guilt out of the minds of lesser mortals. What a dangerous situation!

A virtuous man alone can use the instrument of conscience. He alone can hear the inner voice of the soul clearly. In a wicked man this faculty is dead. The sensitive nature of his conscience has been destroyed by sin or corruption. Hence he is unable to discriminate right from wrong. Those who are leading organizations, business enterprises, institutions and governments should develop this virtue or the ability to use their own conscience. This wisdom of using a clean conscience will enable them to enjoy freedom from anxiety and all kinds of worries.

If you do wrong actions and sinful deeds and treat them lightly today, you will not hesitate to perform serious crimes tomorrow. If you allow one sin to enter and dwell in your conscience, you certainly pave the way for the entry of a thousand sins. Your conscience will become blunt and lose its sensitivity. The habit of doing evil deeds will pervade the whole body like the poison of a scorpion.

Do you know when you are corrupt, your children, who are enjoying the fruits of your corruption, are mocking you? After all, they are well informed and knowledgeable. Your parental mask is too thin to hide the contempt of your children. You are no more the role model of your own children. Is this not disgrace enough?

Our society is fast reaching a stage where the conscience of people holding positions of consequence is being challenged by corruption, just as HIV challenges the physical immunity of an AIDS patient. Corruption has seeped into every stream of our lifeblood. Can we save ourselves as a civilization?

Spiritual leaders have evolved morals, codes and teachings of righteousness. Many beautiful hymns, songs and prayers have been written and composed but the annihilation of conscience by corruption appears frightening. Religion has not been effective in evoking our conscience. Who will, then? Can our conscience be redeemed?

NOBLE THOUGHTS

Once, as I was leaving for Bangalore for a lecture, I spoke to a friend and told him that I would be talking to young people and asked if he had any suggestions. He did not give any suggestion as such but offered me the following words of wisdom:

'When you speak, speak the truth; perform what you promise; discharge your trust. Withhold your hands from striking, and from taking that which is unlawful and bad.

'What actions are most excellent? To gladden the heart of a human being, to feed the hungry, to help the afflicted, to lighten the sorrow of the sorrowful and to remove the wrongs of the injured.

'All God's creatures are His family; and he is the most beloved of God who tries to do most good to God's creatures.'

He told me that these are the sayings of Prophet Mohammed. My friend who told me this is a great-grandson of the Deekshidar of Tamil Nadu and is a Gnanapathigal (Vedic scholar). Such an outlook is possible only in our country where many of our enlightened citizens go beyond their own religion and appreciate other religions also.

There is a beautiful couplet, or kural, in *Thirukkural* by the poet-saint Thiruvalluvar written 2,200 years ago. It means think ever of rising higher. Let it be your only thought. Even if your object be not attained, the thought itself will have raised you.

A NOBLE ACTION

At a sports meet for physically and mentally handicapped children conducted by the National Institute for the Mentally Handicapped, Hyderabad, I witnessed an unforgettable incident. In one race, nine contestants, all physically or mentally disabled, assembled at the starting line for a 100-metre race. At the starting signal, they all started out, not exactly in a dash, but with a relish to run the race to the finish and win. But one little boy stumbled on the asphalt, tumbled over a couple of times, and began to cry. The other eight heard the boy cry. They slowed down and looked back. And then they all turned around and went back, every one of them. One girl with Down's Syndrome bent down and kissed him and said, 'This will make it better.' Then all nine linked their arms together and walked together till they reached the finish line. Everyone in the stadium stood and clapped and the cheering went on for several minutes.

People who were there that day are still telling the story. Why? Because deep down we know this one thing: what matters in this life more than winning for ourselves is helping others win, even if it means slowing down and changing our course. I would say that you do not have to slow down. Rather, by helping others through the difficult areas, the feedback will make you go faster. If you pass this on, we may be able to change our hearts as well as someone else's. A candle loses nothing by lighting another candle.

THE PATH OF RIGHTEOUSNESS

Righteousness of the heart leads to a perfect life of an enlightened citizen. This is beautifully explained by the Chinese philosopher, Confucius, in the ascent and descent phase of human life wherein he states:

> People who desire to have a clear moral harmony in the world would first order their national life; those who desire to order their national life would first regulate their home life; those who desire to regulate their home life would first cultivate their personal life; those who desire to cultivate their personal life and set their heart to righteousness would first make their wills sincere; those who desire to make their wills sincere would first arrive at understanding; understanding comes from the exploration of knowledge of things. When the knowledge of things is gained, then understanding is reached; when understanding is reached, then the will is sincere; when the will is sincere then the heart is righteous; when the heart is righteous then the personal life is cultivated; when the personal life is cultivated, then the home life is regulated; when the home life is regulated, then the national life is orderly; when the national life is orderly then the world is at peace. From the emperor down to the common man, the cultivation of the righteous life is the foundation for all.'

Our righteous toil is our guiding light,
If we work hard, we all can prosper.
Nurture great thoughts, rise up in actions,
May righteous methods be our guide.

E-governance for Transparent Societies

CONNECTIVITY EMPOWERS

Good governance is being recognized as an important goal by countries across the world. Several nations have taken up specific initiatives for open government. Freedom of information is being redefined and supported by detailed guidelines. In this context, the Internet revolution has proved to be a powerful tool for good governance initiatives. The Internet enables the availability of services any time, anywhere.

Along with this there is also a conscious effort to put the citizen as the point of focus in governance. Citizens are being perceived as customers and clients and delivery of services to citizens is now being considered as a primary function of the government.

In a democratic nation of over a billion people such as India, e-governance will enable seamless access to information and, in a federal set-up such as ours, ensure the flow of information from the state to the Centre and vice versa.

TRUST AND CONFIDENCE IN GOVERNANCE

As a function of governance, the government needs to provide multiple facilities and services to its people. These services also require to be constantly upgraded with the use of technology for fulfilling the changing needs and aspirations of the people. The government budgets and expends a large amount of funds for fulfilling this goal. In its Five Year Plans, it allocates a million crore for national development. The money for this work comes from the people, through taxes, to be spent for the benefit of all people, particularly the needy.

However, when it comes to the benefits reaching the common man, the value of the services that reaches the citizen is much below expectations. This happens in all service sectors, namely education, healthcare, sanitation, water, power, infrastructure and tele-communication, as well as in many other areas of importance such as the seeking of loans from the banks for agriculture and small-scale industries. Citizens even have to struggle for the timely payment for certain services and sometimes have to adopt wrong means for making the payment.

The government is responsible for the betterment of the lives of the people by enacting appropriate policies and laws and by facilitating societal transformation. The success of the policies the government enacts varies with the management style adopted by it. Our people have shown enormous resilience and have achieved phenomenal success when provided with an environment of trust and confidence. Whenever there has been a programme run on mission mode, through a specially conceived management structure, we have seen very satisfactory results, whether in governmental or quasi-governmental or private sectors.

THE CONCEPT OF E-GOVERNANCE

I visualize e-governance as this: A transparent, smart system of governance with seamless access and secure and authentic flow of information that crosses inter-departmental barriers and provides fair and unbiased service to the citizens.

I have always been an advocate of using technology for the betterment of our society. E-governance is one such opportunity. But I would like all of you to remember that technology is a double-edged sword. If we don't have an implementation plan from concept to completion, technology becomes expensive and we will not be able to properly reap the benefits. Hence, it is essential for the nation to implement the e-governance process fast. While doing this, we must also have a quantitative measure of the impact of e-governance on our society. Every year, we must be able to measure the number of people who have been touched by the benefits of e-governance.

BENEFITS OF COMPUTERIZATION

Perhaps many of my younger readers do not even remember the manner in which we had to make train, bus and air ticket reservations a few decades ago. We had to stand in long queues a couple of months before the date of travel (for train tickets) or visit the airline office and bus stations. Now, with the advent of Internet and mobile-based reservation systems, we are able to get this work done with minimum wastage of time. Transactions are clean and hassle-free and we can do this while on the move as well.

Similarly, the benefits of Internet-based payment of telephone and electricity bills implemented by many telephone and electricity boards have led to ease for customers. Our voters' cards are now made available to us by applying through forms that can be downloaded from the Election Commission's websites and by following the instructions available on the site.

All of these are examples of ways in which people are not only able to complete the tasks with ease, but do so without involving middlemen and thus reducing the avenues for harassment and corruption.

TRANSPARENCY IN E-GOVERNANCE

Today's information technology and communication systems have ended all concerns of time and distance. There is a new paradigm in this system of democratization of information: one where information can be accessed at any time from anywhere in the world.

India needs to transform into a transparent society and, for that, it is essential that government functions which have public interface or interactions—especially where the state and central functionaries have to provide correct information—be done through the tools of information technology and communication. This means that software has to be written to codify the rules and procedures of government functions, which the public can then access. Only then can we provide equal access to all, and even exceptions to the rules can be made in a transparent manner.

Since India's core competence is in information technology and communication, transparency in administration and management through e-commerce and e-business, leading to e-governance, is definitely possible. Actions have to be initiated in mission mode. An appropriate legal system should also be in place to validate such modes of interactions.

SOME VISIBLE GOOD GOVERNANCE PRACTICES

Now I would like to discuss some of the visible practices of good and transparent governance as practised by the three pillars of our democracy.

Legislative System: The passing of the Right to Education Act 2009, the Right to Information Act 2005, and the National Rural Employment Guarantee Act 2005 are some examples of the effective functioning of the legislative system. These Acts are structured to fulfill a part of the aspirations of our citizens.

Executive System: Some of the key accomplishments of the executive system have been the time-bound realization of the metro railway system in Delhi; the successful, though partial, implementation of e-governance models in certain states, bringing about substantial transparency in the system; a working model of the railway reservation system; the virtual university initiatives of the three 150-year-old universities of the country, namely Madras, Calcutta and Mumbai; and the healthcare services provided through the Yeshaswini scheme. Innovative monitoring systems for electrical energy generation and distribution, leading to the reduction of losses and pilferage, have made a few state electricity boards profitable institutions.

Judicial System: Delay in justice also adds to corruption. I am extremely happy to see that our judicial system has risen to take on this challenge well. I was also very happy to see certain cases where justice was administered speedily. These are good models to emulate for a speedy justice delivery system. However, there are millions of cases pending in different courts for justice. An e-governance judicial system should enable categorization and priority allocation for the speedy disposal of cases.

The judgements of the Supreme Court and some high courts are now available on the Internet. This step has considerably relieved the agony of the litigants and also enables others to use these judgements in their areas of interest. This is a giant step towards transparency. It is essential that all other courts in the country also follow this model. They need to be facilitated by the law ministry, the state governments and the higher judiciary in these endeavours. In addition to this, landmark directions from the Supreme Court on the use of CNG, and the interlinking of rivers will also have a large impact on the welfare of the society.

Litigation-Free Villages: I would like to recall one of my experiences when I was in Chitrakoot, Madhya Pradesh, some years ago. I met a great man, of whom many of you might have heard about. He is the famous ninety-year-old social activist, Dr Nanaji Deshmukh. He was instrumental in making eighty villages 'litigation free' through the DRI (Deendayal Research Institute). This was a successful experiment for resolving disputes within families and within villages. Nanaji said he aimed to create a beautiful society, an empowered society and, above all, a society with moral values.

So it is possible to create a corruption-free society by enlisting good human beings, and spreading the message of their success.

SOME NATIONAL CHALLENGES

One of our nation's biggest challenges is the upliftment of the 270 million people who are below the poverty line. They need housing, food, healthcare, and they need education and employment, which will enable them to lead a good life. Our GDP is oscillating between 4-6 per cent per annum, whereas economists suggest that to uplift the people living below the poverty line, our economy has to grow at the rate of 10 per cent per annum consistently for over a decade.

INTEGRATED ACTION FOR DEVELOPMENT

To meet the needs of over one billion people, our primary mission should be to transform India into a developed nation. There are five areas where India has core competencies for integrated action: (1) Agriculture and food processing (2) Reliable and quality electric power, surface transport and infrastructure for all parts of the country (3) Education and healthcare (4) Information and communication technology (5) Strategic sectors. These five areas are closely inter-related and when effectively addressed, would lead to food, economic, energy and national security.

To implement programmes in an integrated way as well as in a time-bound and cost-effective fashion in order to provide necessary services to the citizens equitably, and with ease, it is essential that we use the technology available to us today and work out a comprehensive e-governance system for all government-to-government and government-to-citizens transactions.

No country has so far implemented an e-governance system for over one billion people. Therefore, it is a big challenge for us.

THE IDEAL SCENARIO

As an example of the use of technology in the democratic process, I visualize an election scenario where a candidate files his nomination from a particular constituency. Immediately, the election officer verifies the authenticity from the national citizen ID database through a multipurpose citizen ID card. The candidate's civic consciousness and citizenship behaviour can also be accessed through the police crime records. The property records come from land registration authorities across the country. Income and wealth resources come from the income tax department, as well as other sources. The person's education credentials come from his university records. The track record of employment comes from various employers with whom he has worked. The credit history comes from various credit institutions like banks. The person's legal track records come from the judicial system. All the details arrive at the computer terminal of the election officer within a few minutes through the e-governance software, which would track various state and central government web services directories through the network and collect the information quickly and automatically and present facts in real-time without any bias. An artificial intelligence software would analyse the candidate's credentials and give a rating on how successful that person would be as a politician. The election officer can then make an informed choice and start the electoral processes.

Is this a dream? Is this possible? If possible, by when can we implement it? Can we provide good governance to over one billion people? Can e-governance speed up the delivery system? Can e-governance differentiate between genuine transactions and spurious transactions? Can e-governance ensure immediate action for genuine cases and stop action on spurious transactions? Can this be done by e-governance at a cost affordable by our nation?

CHALLENGES OF E-GOVERNANCE

I will now try to seek an answer for the questions I asked by asking another set of questions. Do we have the framework required for e-governance? Do we have a national citizen database that will be the primary source of information for all governance across state and central governments? Do we have standards for the exchange of secure information with non-repudiation across state and central government departments seamlessly? Do we have a secure delivery framework, that is, a virtual private network that connects state and central government departments across the country? Do we have data centres in central and state governments to handle the departmental workflow automation, collaboration, interaction, and the exchange of information with authentication? Should our administrative systems be empowered and reformed so that they can accelerate decision-making processes? When will the entire administrative body be able to contribute more towards national development rather than entangling itself in bureaucratic processes?

Let us try to find an answer to each of the above questions by asking ourselves: How can we evolve such a system? Let me focus on the Societal Grid Model proposed by me to ensure overall inclusive development by connecting the various domains that will make a visible impact on the quality of life of the people.

CONNECTIVITY MODEL: SOCIETAL GRID

In the proposed model, the Knowledge Grid, the Rural (PURA) Grid, the Health Grid and the Governance Grid is a system of multiple portals. This system of grids will bring prosperity to about 843 million people in rural areas and about 343 million people in urban areas. In the process, it will ensure that the lives of the people below the poverty line are transformed.

First let me talk about the Knowledge Grid. For bridging the rural and urban divide and ensuring the equitable distribution of prosperity, India needs to be connected. The core of this connectivity model is the partnership between governmental and other institutions both in public and private domains. The strength of this partnership is facilitated by the free flow of knowledge and information.

THE KNOWLEDGE GRID

The endeavour here is to transform an information society into a knowledge society. The knowledge society will be a society producing, marketing and using products and services that are rich in both explicit and tacit knowledge, thus creating value-added products for national and international consumption. In the knowledge economy, the objective of a society changes from merely fulfilling the basic needs of all-round development to *empowerment*. For instance, the education system, instead of going by textbook teaching, will promote creative and interactive self-learning—both formal and informal—with a focus on values, merit and quality. Workers, instead of being skilled or semi-skilled, will be knowledgeable, self-empowered and flexibly skilled. Types of work, instead of being structured and hardware driven, will be more flexible and software driven. Management styles will be delegative rather than directive. In this model, the impact on environment and ecology will also be strikingly less compared to the industrial economy model. The economy itself will be knowledge driven. The key infrastructure required for this is telecom and all related tools of communication such as computers and software.

In this model, it is essential to provide equitable access to an education system that moves beyond the classroom. The bandwidth is a demolisher of imbalances and a great leveller in a knowledge society. We have rich knowledge institutions but what we need is connectivity. This connectivity is technologically possible today but would require the creation of a reliable network infrastructure, with a high bandwith of at least 10 Gigabits per second, all through the country, to provide uniform access of knowledge in different regions, leading to the creation of the Knowledge Grid.

INTER-CONNECTING UNIVERSITIES WITH SOCIO-ECONOMIC INSTITUTIONS, INDUSTRIES AND R&D ORGANIZATIONS

India is planning to connect 5,000 institutions across the country with a Gigabit network for the creation of a collaborative knowledge-sharing platform. Three of India's 150-year-old universities, namely, the University of Madras, the University of Calcutta and the University of Mumbai, have created a 'Virtual University' to provide ten unique joint post-graduate programmes to students of these three universities thus providing quality education without regional affiliations. India has also embarked upon the mission of providing quality education services to fifty-three African nations by connecting its seven universities.

THE HEALTHCARE GRID

This is based on inter-connecting the healthcare institutions of government, corporate and super speciality hospitals, as well as research institutions, educational institutions and ultimately, pharma R&D institutions. India has connected around 300 remote locations so far, with more than forty-five super speciality hospitals, and provides tele-medicine connectivity. In addition, programmes for providing healthcare services to fifty-three African nations by connecting twelve super speciality hospitals from India as a part of the Pan-African e-Network is in progress.

Healthcare training institutes, which include nurses, para-medical staff and doctors, and medical research institutions, should also be added to the Health Grid. This will enable unique case studies and experiences to be exchanged between healthcare institutions. It will also be possible to conduct conferences where specialist doctors from various remote centres can discuss critical disease patterns and provide treatment.

THE E-GOVERNANCE GRID

Inter-connecting the central and state governments as well as district- and block-level offices for G2G and G2C connectivity is part of the E-governance Grid. India is creating State Wide Area Network (SWAN) across the country and has fibre connectivity up to the block level.

THE PURA KNOWLEDGE GRID

This grid is the backbone for rural development. All other grids will infuse knowledge into this grid for sustainable development, healthcare and good governance. Through the PURA Grid, integrated Common Service Centres will act as an inter-connected delivery mechanism for tele-education, tele-medicine and e-governance services besides individual access by people within and between village knowledge centres.

VILLAGE KNOWLEDGE CENTRES

For providing knowledge connectivity to the PURA Grid, village knowledge centres will act as the front-line delivery system. I visualize the establishment of village knowledge centres in village panchayats to empower villagers with knowledge and to act as a local centre for knowledge connectivity within the overall framework of PURA. The village knowledge centre should provide essential data required for targeted populations, such as farmers, fishermen, craftsmen, traders, businessmen, entrepreneurs, unemployed youths and students. One million Common Service Centres (CSC) have been set up across the country through public-private partnership to address these issues.

The main focus of the CSC is not only to provide information and e-governance but also to empower the youth to undertake development tasks in the villages and establish rural enterprises, which, in turn, will lead to large-scale rural employment. So, it is essential to skill-enable and knowledge-enable with the help of academic institutions, industry, banking and marketing institutions. The CSC should act as a facilitator.

PURA NODAL KNOWLEDGE DATA CENTRE

Kisan Call Centres provide valuable and timely knowledge support to farmers and fishermen. Similar domain service provider call centres are required in the field of commerce and industry, entrepreneurial skill development and employment generation, travel and tourism, banking and insurance, meteorological forecasting, disaster warning systems, education and human resource development and healthcare.

These call centres will act as service providers to the PURA Nodal Knowledge Data Centres located in the PURA complexes which, in turn, will provide area specific and customized knowledge to the village knowledge centres (or CSCs) in the villages in a holistic manner. This delivery will depend on the availability of robust connectivity in different parts of the country. The PURA Grid, then, will draw information from the other Grids and will act as a catalyst for societal transformation in rural areas.

The Effects of Corruption

CERTAIN EXPERIENCES IN GOVERNANCE

It is well known that in government schemes and welfare projects, there is sometimes fictitious reporting or the full money allotted is shown as spent and claims of objectives being fully met are not backed up by proper evidence to corroborate the claims.

Thus we can see that in the absence of a non-transparent system, a well-intentioned programme fails to produce the desired results. This clearly shows the effect of corruption on governance and the failure of our system to protect the human rights of citizens.

The next area I would like to touch upon is the corruption level as reported in different states based on certain studies.

The levels vary from one state to next and the reasons for this should be established. Can it be due to political awareness? Can it be due to better Human Development Index? Can it be due to an alert media? Can it be due to women's empowerment? It may be useful to study these aspects and assess the possible reasons, so that they can be emulated by other states.

IDENTIFYING THE HEROES

In any village or panchayat or district, we will always find at least a few corruption-free good human beings. We may even find pockets of corruption-free societies. If these can be identified and celebrated, we can create a nearly corruption-free state. The real-world examples of corruption-free individuals and groups and societies must be discussed publicly, so that they can become examples to be followed in the country. A nation can be corruption free only when its states are corruption free; a state can be corruption free only if its districts are corruption free; a district can be corruption free only if its panchayats are corruption free; a panchayat can be corruption free only if the people are corruption free; and people can be corruption free only if they have imbibed these values from their childhood.

CERTAIN EXPERIENCES IN SOCIETAL LIFE

The creation of a corruption-free society depends heavily on the environment at home, the school, the society and the government, besides on the individual. Let me discuss the various components of this complex fabric.

CORRUPTION-FREE SOCIETY STARTS AT HOME

On 21 November 2005, I visited Adichunchanagiri Math to attend a function of the Foundation for Unity of Religions and Enlightened Citizenship and I interacted with over 54,000 students of various schools and colleges of Karnataka. There, a tenth-standard student, M. Bhavani, studying at Adichunchanagiri Composite High School, Shimoga, asked me the following question: 'Sir, I would like to be a citizen of a corruption-free nation. Please tell me, as a student, how can I contribute?'

The agony of a young mind is reflected in this question. For me, it was an important question, since it came from a young person. As I thought about what answer I could give her, my thoughts were as follows:

There are over a billion people in the country and nearly 200 million homes. In general, there are good citizens everywhere. However, if we find that the people in a few million houses are not transparent and not amenable to the laws of the country, what can we do? This is where young people come in: they are the ones who can eradicate corruption from its base, that is, the home. If the parents in these houses are deviating from the honest path then the children need to guide their parents or their elders on to the right path with love, affection and encouragement.

I told all the children assembled at that gathering that in case their parents were deviating from the path of transparency and honesty, they needed to speak up and boldly take their parents to task, reminding them that they taught their children right from wrong, and were, therefore, setting a bad example. Most of the children spontaneously responded, 'We will do it.'

Similarly, I have also told parents the same thing in another meeting. Initially there was silence, but later, many of them hesitantly agreed that they would abide by the children's suggestion since it was driven by love. They took an oath in front of me. It was: 'I will lead an honest life free from all corruption and will set an example for others to adopt a transparent way of life.'

Finally I told the students that they should start a movement against corruption that begins at their home. I am confident that children can reform their families.

THE MISSION OF THE TEACHER

School is the next important environment where character is shaped. The prime learning period for children is between five to seventeen years of age. Through the learning years, the student spends approximately 25,000 hours at the school campus. Hence school hours are the best time for learning, making it crucial that the school has the best of environment: mission-oriented learning with a value system in place. As Bestolozzy, a Greek teacher, said, 'Give me a child for seven years. Afterwards, let the God or the devil take the child. They cannot change the child.'

That is the great confidence of the teacher. What a mission for teachers to build character and inculcate high morals in the students of the country!

ELEVATING YOUNG MINDS

The next component I would like to discuss is the importance of moral classes for students in order to elevate their minds. While I was in college, I remember the lectures given by the highest authority of the Jesuit institution, Rev. Father Rector Kalathil of St. Joseph's College, Tiruchirapalli. Every Monday, he would take an hour-long class. He talked about good human beings of the present and the past, and what creates goodness in human beings. In this class, he would give lectures on personalities such as the Buddha, Confucius, St. Augustine, Khalifa Omar, Mahatma Gandhi, Einstein, Abraham Lincoln and several others as well as moral stories linked to our civilizational heritage. He also talked about great personalities who had made huge contributions towards the service of the people.

It is essential in secondary schools and colleges to arrange for lectures by great teachers once a week on such topics. This will elevate young minds and teach them to love their country, to love other human beings and inculcate noble values in them.

CODE OF CONDUCT

The fourth important component for promoting a transparent society is forming an informal code of conduct for people in high places of responsibility. Here I am reminded of a line from a Tamil classic, which brings out the power of righteousness and provides a code of conduct for the people in high and responsible positions. It says that if people who are in high and responsible positions go against righteousness, righteousness itself will be transformed into a destroyer. Whoever deviates from righteousness, whether they are the individual or the state, is responsible for their own actions. This message is mentioned very clearly by Ilango Adigal in *Silappathikaram*, one of the five great Tamil epics written nearly 2,000 years ago.

So far, I have been talking about the strategies needed for the creation of enlightened citizens. Now I would like to discuss transparency in governance, which is one of the primary requirements of the democratic system.

TRUST AND CONFIDENCE IN GOVERNANCE

We have to imagine a scene. I call it 'A Scene of Sweat'. It is the farmer in the agricultural field, the fisherman in the rough sea, the worker in the factory, the teacher in the school, the knowledge worker in the laboratory, the health worker in healthcare institutions and many, many others who have to be remembered when we take a political, administrative or judicial decision. I would consider a government machinery corruption free only if the purpose for which the machinery has been set up is fulfilled, in letter and in spirit, with honesty, sincerity and purposefulness.

HOW TO CREATE A CORRUPTION-FREE SOCIETY

Some of the methodologies here would be the introduction of a robust system of e-governance.

E-governance has already shown its impact in our legislative, executive and judicial systems. In the legislative system, the Right to Education Act 2009, the Right to Information Act 2005, and the National Rural Employment Guarantee Act 2005 are some of the recent examples of the effective functioning of the legislative system. In the executive system, we have implemented partial e-governance in certain states, including a working railway reservation system, and the creation of a virtual university through the combined efforts of three universities of the country. In the judiciary, implementation of e-governance has led to the speedy resolution of several cases. The judgements of the Supreme Court and some high courts are now available on the Internet.

A corruption-free society is not merely a dream, it is entirely achievable. All we need is the role of the enlightened citizen in the creation of a method of governance that promotes transparency and honesty for the better functioning of democracy.

Conscience is the light of the soul. It raises its voice in protest whenever anything that is contrary to truth and righteousness is thought of or done. Conscience is a form of truth that has been transferred through our genetic stock in the form of knowledge of our own acts and feelings as right or wrong. Only a virtuous and courageous person can use the instrument of conscience and that person alone can clearly hear the inner voice of the soul. In a wicked person, this faculty is dead. The sensitive nature of the conscience gets destroyed by sin or corruption and the person is unable to discriminate right from wrong. Those who are leading organizations, business enterprises, institutions and governments should develop this virtue: the ability to use their own conscience.

The Vision for a New India

Many civilizations collapsed and many nations failed because they did not have the vision at the right time.

In the last many years, I have met seventeen million youth in all parts of the country. Some incidents from these interactions stand out in my mind.

DYNAMICS OF THE MIND OF THE YOUTH

On 19 Jan 2011, I visited Amravati to attend a programme organized by the Satpuda Shikshan Prasarak Mandal to address one lakh youth. I gave a talk, 'I am Unique', in the presence of many political and societal development leaders, teachers and educationists. After I finished my lecture, among many other questions, an interesting question came from a rural boy.

He introduced himself as a tenth-standard student from Harali village. He asked, 'Sir, our media and my friends always say that China's economy is progressing better and faster than India. Tell me, sir, why can't India's develop faster? Also tell us what we, the youth, should do?'

There was great applause for this boy's question, which meant that the crowd of one lakh young people needed a right answer from me. My friends on the dais, too, were looking to me for an answer. Reflecting for a brief moment, I asked the boy what his name was. He said his name was Vineet. I said, 'Vineet, you have a powerful mind and you also love your nation. My answer to you is: it is true that the economic progress made by China and India are reportedly quite

143

different. But India is following a system of parliamentary democracy, elected by the people. Democracy has its ups and downs, but we must keep flying. The associated delays have to be removed through good leadership. But I want to ask all the youth assembled here, suppose I give two systems: one with full democracy and with a high pace of development, and the other, a political system like China's, which one would you like to choose?'

When I asked them to raise their hands, 99 per cent of the youth raised their hands and said that they wanted a democracy with a faster rate of growth.

The message here is that the youth want democracy to be re-invented with faster growth. The young mind is turbulent and looking for a vision for the nation and its fast accomplishment. It is very important to engage young minds with an inspiring vision for thinking and action.

'WHEN CAN I SING A SONG OF INDIA?'

During the last few years, I have seen how the India Vision 2020 has inspired people, particularly the youth of the nation.

I recall a situation in 1990 where I was interacting with the youth of Ahmedabad. One girl there asked me a question, 'When can I sing a song of India?' At that time, her brother, who was in the United States, was always talking about how the United States was best at everything. This girl sitting in India was fed up with her brother's stories and, in her quest to find an answer, asked, 'When can I sing a song of India?'

How did I answer? I explained to her the India Vision 2020 and told her, 'Have confidence and certainly you can sing a song of India by 2020.'

But, for the last few years, while interacting with the youth, I have been seeing a marked change in the thinking. From a notion of what can the nation offer me, they have been asking me, 'What can I give to the nation?' That means the youth are ready to contribute towards national development. Recently, I have observed a further change. There is more confidence among our young people. For instance, during my address in Shillong in 2013, a youth told me, 'I can do it, we can do it and the nation can do it.' With the youth actively participating in the developmental process, I am sure that India will be transformed into a developed nation before the year 2020.

I would like to focus on three aspects of this participation for the youth in governance: the birth of a vision, the current ambience in India and its challenges and, finally, the mission to graduate the nation into an economically developed nation.

THE BIRTH OF A VISION

Let me share with you my unique experience of the formulation of the Vision 2020 strategies in the mid-1990s. I was given the task of chairing the Technology Information, Forecasting and Assessment Council (TIFAC). I recollect that in the first meeting of the council, we took a decision that the TIFAC must evolve a plan as to how India can be transformed into an economically developed nation by the year 2020. When the suggestion was mooted, everybody wondered how we could evolve such a long-term mission under the prevailing economic and social conditions of the country. That was the time when Prime Minister Narasimha Rao had just announced the economic liberalization and growth measures for the Indian economy and its impact was starting to be felt.

In spite of this, the council, with many young members, jumped to the idea and we discussed for one full day how we could translate thought into action. At a time when the economy was growing at around 5 to 6 per cent per annum in GDP, we had to envisage a growth rate of at least 10 per cent per annum consistently for over ten years for realizing the development vision of 2020. This challenge ignited the minds of all of us in the council. The members of the TIFAC council at that time included the principal secretary to the prime minister, the nine secretaries to the government of India, the chiefs of CII, ASSOCHAM and FICCI, the chairman of IDBI, ICICI, IFCI, the chairman of public sector corporations, the chief executives of a number of private sector institutions, the vice chancellors of different universities and scientists from the Department of Science and Technology. We debated and arrived at seventeen task teams with over 500 members, who consulted with over 5,000 people in various sectors of the economy.

Committees worked for over two years, resulting in twenty-five reports which we presented to the then prime minister on 2 August 1996. The reports included vision on areas such as agro-food processing, advance sensors, civil aviation, electric power, waterways, road transportation, tele-communications, food and agriculture, engineering industries, healthcare, life science and biotechnology, materials and processing, electronics and communications, chemical process industry, services, strategic industry and driving forces. Transforming India into a developed nation implied that every citizen of the country would live well above the poverty line, their education and health would be of a high standard, national security would be assured and core competence in certain major areas would enable production of quality goods competitively for export and for bringing all-round prosperity for countrymen.

IMPEDIMENTS TO THE NATIONAL VISION

As I see it, some of the impediments to Vision 2020 are as follows:

The vision document was prepared at the time of Prime Minister Narasimha Rao. The document was given to Prime Minister Atal Bihari Vajpayee. Vajpayeeji announced in the Parliament and also announced during his Independence Day address at the Red Fort that India will become an economically developed nation before 2020. In the governors' conference during my presidency, Prime Minister Manmohan Singh also announced that his government would work for an economically developed nation and he assured all the governors of the states.

My experience says that Vision 2020 does not belong to a party, a government or an individual. It is the national vision. It has to be discussed in detail by all elected representatives of the nation for a few weeks in the Parliament and they should debate, discuss and assent so that a national consensus will emerge within all the stakeholders of the vision—including the executive, the judiciary, political leaders, the media, the academia, the business industry, the medical community, farmers, the youth and the people of the nation. For this reason, there should be a commitment towards the national vision from every individual in all walks of life.

If it takes fifteen years for the realization of such a vision document, it means that three democratically elected governments have to work together to realize this vision, although the methodology may be different. National missions cannot be a part of a party agenda, but it *can* be a part of its election manifesto and should be realized. The vision needs to be approved by the Parliament, so that there will remain a continuity in its progress, irrespective of the period of the three governments.

Hence the elected leader of the nation should be a creative leader, who walks the path of pursuing developmental politics, adopting cooperation and collaboration as the key to operational procedure and using the core competence of all parties—irrespective of party affiliations—as well as other able and creative minds from any discipline to realize the vision of an economically developed nation.

CURRENT AMBIENCE IN INDIA

Now, let me provide a visualization of India as an economically developed India by the year 2020. The Indian economy was growing at an average of 9 per cent per annum till the year 2008. In 2009-10, the Indian economy was affected due to global economic turbulence, but nevertheless grew at over 7 per cent in the year of global recession. Even when the economic zones of the US and the Europe still looked bleak, India grew at about 6.9 per cent in the last quarter of 2011. In 2013, the GDP growth was at the 5.5 per cent mark.

I was asking myself what type of innovation is needed to enrich the Indian economy and other world economies under the present circumstances. I had discussions on this subject with several economic experts. It came to light that the Indian economy can withstand the world financial crisis better. This is due to:

- The liberalization process in India has checks and balances consistent with the unique social requirements of the country.
- The Indian banking system has always been conservative, which has prevented a crisis similar to that in the US and in Europe.
- The Indian psyche is generally savings-oriented and living within one's means is a part of the Indian mindset.
- The 400-million-strong middle class, with its purchasing power, is providing economic stability to the nation.

Therefore, India is able to withstand the global economic crisis to a certain extent, but we are still vulnerable to the vagaries of the global economic turbulence because of an excess of imports and reduced exports, leading to trade deficit, increased current account deficit—which leads to inflation—and the depreciation of the rupee to 60.49 per US dollar in June 2013. If the US banks fail, the Indian economy is affected. If the EU faces an economic crisis, we see its effect on the Indian economy.

Why does this happen even though India has a good economic foundation? It is because we have an economic system which is vulnerable to the fluctuations of the world economy and our economic growth is not sustainable, as witnessed from the 5 per cent GDP growth in the 1990s to 9 per cent for around four years till 2009 and, finally, the present 5.5 per cent. This is mainly due to our prevailing economic policies which are stifling the growth of agriculture and food processing, the manufacturing sector and the service sector. If we bring a marked change in our socio-political and economic policies with a focus on inclusiveness, then I am confident that we as a nation will be able to overcome the economic crisis and progress to new heights.

WHAT HAS INDIA ACHIEVED?

We have only six years left in order to achieve the goals of Vision 2020. The nation should take this as its primary task, and facilitate all stakeholders to contribute towards realizing the goals of this mission.

The India Vision 2020 is progressing; today India has made substantial progress in enhancing agricultural productivity and increasing per capita income. According to NASSCOM, the IT–BPO sector in India aggregated revenues of US $100 billion in FY2012, where export and domestic revenue stood at US $69.1 billion and US $31.7 billion respectively, growing by over 9 per cent. The pharma industry has grown to US $20 billion. The ISRO-enabled mission to find water on the moon through Chandrayaan-1 was undertaken and the Mars Orbiter Mission has reached the orbit of the Red Planet. India is the world's second-largest mobile phone user with 900 million users. The Indian automobile industry has become the third largest in the world with 2.8 million automobile vehicles produced in 2013.

Large-scale infrastructure has also been created as a part of rural and urban development missions such as the multi-lane Golden Quadrilateral roadways and the development of airport infrastructure in all metro cities. All rural roads are getting developed at the state level as well.

The current literacy rate in India stands at 74.04 per cent. India's healthcare sector is projected to grow to nearly US$ 40 billion and quality healthcare infrastructure is projected to reach all states by 2015. We are also aspiring to provide clean, green energy and safe drinking water to all the citizens of the nation.

With this growth, we have to assess where we are in terms of what we aspired to in the 1990s, and where the gap is. It is time for the nation and its leaders to take up a review mission to assess the gap and suggest methods by which we can accelerate progress so that, by 2020, India can become a developed country with:

- Zero poverty;
- 100 per cent literacy;
- Quality healthcare for all;
- Value-systems embedded quality education for all;
- Value-added employment for every citizen consistent with education and professional skills.

If we channelize our integrated efforts towards the development of India before 2020, then the growth of the nation is certain.

ECONOMICALLY DEVELOPED NATION AND ITS MISSIONS

Based on my interaction with various intellectuals, experts and researchers from universities in India and abroad and students and faculty from IIMs Ahmedabad, Indore, Bangalore and Shillong and with the millions of students of the nation, let me propose the following action points for realizing our goal of an economically developed nation:

SUSTAINABLE RURAL DEVELOPMENT

PURA: Based on both private institutional and government efforts, PURA has become a proven model for sustainable rural development. Hence, for bringing all-round sustainable development, India needs to launch the Integrated National PURA Mission to create 7,000 PURA clusters across the nation which will empower Indians and bring sustainable development in rural and urban areas. Every year, we spend more than ₹100,000 crores for national development. Part of those funds can be directed towards realizing the 7,000 PURA clusters.

ENERGY INDEPENDENCE, CLEAN AND GREEN ENVIRONMENT AND WATER MANAGEMENT

Energy: It is essential for the Indian Parliament to announce the 'Energy Independence Mission by 2030'. Power generation through renewable energy has to be increased from 5 per cent to 28 per cent. Dependence on fossil fuels as primary energy source needs to be brought under 50 per cent from the present 75 per cent. Mandating the use of ethanol from 10 per cent to 20 per cent and the associated public policy for ethanol development by the sugarcane industry is also required. There is also a need for a sustainable biofuel policy for generating 60 million tonnes of biofuel, along with the use of alternate sources such as emulsification, bio-algae and hydrogen fuel.

Environment: Enacting an inclusive environment enrichment policy instead of the prevailing extractive environment protection policy is required. We also need to increase the forest cover from 20 per cent to 40 per cent by 2020 as well as enrich the environment through mandatory zero liquid discharge and zero effluent discharge system policies for industrial waste, encourage power generation from biomass and municipal waste at city corporations and village municipalities and create 200,000 carbon-neutral village panchayats before 2020.

Waterways: We need the implementation of the Smart Waterways Grid across India to harness 1,500 BCM of floodwater and connect the rivers and catchment areas as a single plane. The grid will receive 1,500 BCM of floodwater and act as a water grid so that water can be released to any deficient place and replenished during flood. It would act as a 15,000 kilometres-long national reservoir. It would be able to provide drinking water to 600 million people, irrigation to 150 million acres of land, and generate 60,000 MW of power. Due to ground water recharge, it would also save 4,000 MW of power. Each state can implement this mission with an outlay of approximately ₹50,000 crores with annual budgetary support, central government assistance, public-private consortia and with support from the World Bank in a BOOT (Build, Operate, Own and Transfer) based PPP model and this can be realized within 2020.

Apart from this, an Integrated Water Resource Management system is also required to revive water bodies and tanks and build farm ponds and checkdams across India as well as increase irrigation infrastructure and groundwater potential, thereby enhancing the safe drinking water resources of the nation.

THE AGRICULTURE, MANUFACTURING AND SERVICE SECTORS

Agriculture: In this sector, we need to launch the Second Green Revolution mission as an integrated agriculture, industry and service sector programme with an aim of 10 per cent growth rate in agriculture before 2020 and produce a minimum of 340 million tonnes of food as opposed to the present 250 million tonnes despite reduced water, land and human power environment. Technologies such as SSI (Sustainable Sugarcane Initiative) and SRI (System of Rice Intensification), precision farming, a system-oriented approach and technologically advanced pre- and post-harvesting equipment usage will more than double agricultural productivity and ensure the 30 per cent contribution to the GDP by 2020 from the present 15 per cent.

The introduction of the innovative Community Cooperative Farming Model for identifying crops in selected regions based on the characterization of the soil conditions and ensuring that quality input material is available at the right time will also be beneficial. The industry sector has to be empowered with inclusive growth-oriented policies to set up farm-level silos, cold chain, refrigerated transportation, food processing industries, etc.

Manufacturing: The manufacturing industry has to be empowered in order to achieve a 25 per cent GDP contribution by 2020 from the 16 per cent as of 2012. A proactive National Manufacturing Policy is the need of the hour.

It is essential to restructure viable industries with technology, business processes and human resources. Proactive public policy is essential to relieve financial stress, provide liquidity support and save the productive assets of the country.

We need Global Skill Development for the youth to take up value-added employment in the manufacturing and service sectors. An inclusive policy for the adoption of state-of-the-art technology, machines and standards by the industry is essential. Ensuring the availability of energy, capital and logistic transportation for reducing production cost and thereby making the product competitive in the global market will lead to a reduction of inflation. Establishing innovation ecosystems is essential for the growth of the manufacturing and service industries.

EDUCATION AND HEALTHCARE

School Education: Quality input generates quality output. The primary foundation for such action is the quality of teachers at the school level—from the primary to the higher-secondary level. The creation of a revamped National Quality Teacher Education System and its associated inclusive policy is essential. What we need is a creative syllabus, creative teachers and creative classrooms for value-based quality school education.

Higher Education: The higher education system has to focus on research and development at the university level. Instead of monitoring and control by agencies such as the UGC and the AICTE, we should allow higher educational institutions to compete internationally by setting their educational standards at par with world-class institutions so that they can be rated by independent agencies with a pool of eligible experts in the field on rotation. A minimum criteria may be set up for achieving excellence.

Research and Development in Higher Education: Removing red tapism and favoritism in higher education and research administration and management is of utmost importance. We need to empower universities, both government funded and private, to promote research and enable them to improve research infrastructure. Establishing a National Research and Innovation Laboratory with access to all educational institutions at the state and central level is important. Incentives can also be provided to empower professors and students for research and development.

Good faculty attracts good research students. We need to attract a world-class research faculty by creating a world-class working environment, re-envisioning salary structures and providing accommodation in universities for possible collaborative international research projects. Universities should identify national challenges and direct their research towards finding innovative solutions. Every university should set up the PURA Cluster Research Centre for traditional research and development for local application for agriculture, industry and service sectors at the village level.

Healthcare Services and Institutions: More medical colleges should be allowed to start, provided they adopt government hospitals and invest in its infrastructure and health service and also adopt at least a hundred village PHCs (Public Health Centres) in their neighbourhood. Medical teaching may also be imparted through high-definition tele-education technology by a well-qualified faculty and a medical laboratory for practical applications may be tied up with government hospitals.

Comprehensive medical insurance provided by the government to the unorganized sector needs to be introduced to provide quality healthcare service to the common man. The establishment of inclusive policies to set up manufacturing industries for healthcare implements and diagnostic service equipment is also required. Ensuring that quality healthcare reaches all states equally through PHCs, tertiary care, via tele-medicine and also through mobile hospitals should be the primary objective of the nation.

INCLUSIVE GOVERNANCE

Inclusive governance means governance that is responsive, transparent and corruption free. We need to achieve an Ease of Doing Business index to less than 50 compared to its present level of 132. (China is at 91). Introduction of e-governance with dynamic secure workflow management from top to bottom that connects the President, the prime minister, ministries, governors, CMs, state ministries, departments, secretariat, district collectors, village administrative officers and ultimately the people is essential as is the implementation of issuing of national ID to all the citizens.

We also need changes in the Land, Mines and Minerals Act, internal security, police, inclusive industrial reforms, social justice and women's reservation and consider all other pending bills for redefinition with focus on inclusive growth with equitable social justice.

Enacting inclusive polices for regulatory, corporate and moral governance and improving responsiveness and accountability in government initiatives aims to improve government and public sector effectiveness and citizens' engagement with government. A responsible and accountable anti-corruption Lokpal Bill simultaneously builds value systems in both the family and the society. Enacting a Citizen's Charter as a solemn commitment of the government or public sector institutions for delivery of services to the intended beneficiaries on time and every time is also crucial.

REDUCE POVERTY, ILLITERACY AND CRIMES AGAINST WOMEN

The following measures may be taken to bring poverty reduction through PURA for 600,000 villages, which will provide employment opportunities and enrich the quality of life in villages. I have also evolved a User Community Pyramid to ensure that the benefits of the sustainable development model reaches the bottom of the pyramid through the productive use of natural resources, the convergence of technologies, and the evolution of innovative socio-economic business models for evolving a happy, prosperous and peaceful society. We have also developed a radar called the Societal Developmental Radar, which not only provides short-term, mid-term and long-term targets but also monitors the progress of attributes like access to food and nutrition; access to water, both potable and irrigation; access to healthcare; access to income-generation capacity; access to education and capacity building; access to quality power and communication; and access to financial services. This will lead to the intended benefits reaching the bottom of the pyramid.

Skill and knowledge development through state-of-the-art skill training for the youth of the country is also needed. Programmes can be conceived where students from colleges across India would take up a two-month summer internship programme in villages to enhance water and pond conditions and hygiene.

As for women's safety, a value-based education at the school level is essential to build respect towards women. To bring down the rate of crimes, we need to improve police vigilance and put a system in place for immediate FIR on complaints. An SOS call for women may also be introduced through mobile phones or GPS devices.

Inclusive growth-oriented policies will bring equitable, inclusive growth and level socio-economic imbalances in society which will remove socio-economic and political alienation and reduce Naxalist and Maoist tendencies. Developmental politics instead of political politics will also reduce the prevalent bitter political alienation.

BRINGING PEACE AND PROSPERITY

For containing terrorism and other forms of insurgency in India, we need to evolve the NCET (National Campaign to Eradicate Terrorism).

I believe the time has come when, apart from the multiple agencies forecasting and handling terrorist activities, we also need to evolve an aggressive mission called the NCET, with a mission-oriented integrated management structure, duly passed by the Parliament.

Under the NCET Bill, we need to bring out the following:

- Creation of a unified intelligence agency across the country, with the latest technological tools and devices, that is empowered to deal with state and central government intelligence agencies under one roof of administration.
- Enactment of a law which will provide stringent punishment and faster justice to the perpetrators of the crime in a time-bound manner.
- Building wider awareness among people in order to work together in identifying these incidents and eliminating these tendencies with transparent procedures that inform and work with intelligence agencies to combat terrorism.
- Implementation of a national citizen ID card for all transactions with government, business and private sectors.
- Reorientation of central and state administrative mechanisms to ensure that development reaches all sections of the society for achieving inclusive growth and to ensure that no one in the society feels alienated socially, economically and politically.

I have suggested that the evolution of the NCET mission be based around action-oriented people of highest integrity and competence drawn from multiple functional areas, committed to the vision of eradicating terrorism. We must do this with a great sense of urgency for when evil minds combine, good minds have to work together.

REGIONAL PEACE AND PROSPERITY

India should not only work towards bringing sustainable peace and prosperity within its borders but also among its neighbours. India is the second largest democratic nation in the world and its democratic values have been tested for more than six decades. If Vision 2020 has to reap *all* the benefits of development, India has to see that all of its neighbours, particularly the SAARC nations, have attained peace and prosperity under the democratic system. Otherwise cross-border terrorism, Naxalism and Maoism will continue to threaten the very processes of sustaining peace and prosperity. It is the responsibility of India to bring peace and prosperity in the subcontinent through democracy. I suggest that the SAARC nations work together in a way similar to the EU Parliament which works towards promoting regional peace and prosperity.

UNITY OF MINDS

At this point, I would like to suggest that on a social level, it is necessary to work towards the unity of minds. Indian civilization is a multi-lingual, multi-faith, multi-racial system that has evolved over centuries. The increasing intolerance for the views and lifestyle of others and the expression of this intolerance through lawlessness cannot be justified under any context. All of us have to work hard to respect the rights of every individual. That is the most fundamental of all democratic values, and, I believe, our civilizational heritage—the very soul of our nation.

Let us evolve ourselves into a society that respects and celebrates differences. Let our experts, leaders and institutions show in their words and deeds:

* Tolerance of other people's opinions.
* Tolerance of other people's cultures.
* Tolerance of other people's beliefs.
* Tolerance of other people's styles.
* Tolerance of other people's ideas.

In fact, such an attitude, at the individual and community levels, has always been the hallmark of Indian civilization.

POLITICAL SYSTEM IN DEMOCRACY

A democracy works on the foundation of people's dreams and aspirations. It is not democracy that has to be re-invented; what needs to be re-invented is our political system, with its responsibilities, its obligations and its boundaries.

Here I would like to recall my addresses in the Parliament and my address to the fifteen state legislative assemblies on the mission for the development of states. I gave them an equation:

Political system= Political politics + Developmental politics.

Any parliamentarian or legislator has to go through these two political components. Political politics focuses on election and electoral politics, that is, getting elected with a declared agenda. Developmental politics focuses on the development of the constituency as part of the mission to develop the state, and thereby, the nation. This requires vision, measurable mission targets, feedback on progress, and even midcourse corrections whenever necessary. I believe that a member, once elected, should spend only 30 per cent of his time on political politics and the remaining 70 per cent on development politics.

The mission has to be to make the constituency a developed one. The parameters for this are:

1. A constituency free from poverty and crime and where the dignity of every human life in ensured in an unbiased manner.

2. A constituency free from illiteracy with state-of-the-art skill

development and higher education for the youth.

3. Value-added employment for all with enhanced per capita income.

4. Provision of healthcare services to every citizen and eradication of diseases like TB, cholera, malaria, HIV/AIDS and leprosy. Mass screening and provision of proactive healthcare system leading to reduction in IMR, MMR and chronic diseases.

5. Working towards the creation of enduring infrastructure for safe drinking water, drainage, sanitation, irrigation, transportation, power and enhancing the tourism potential of the constituency.

6. Making the process of administration efficient, transparent and corruption free, so that every citizen feels comfortable in receiving services without any hassle and can contribute towards national development.

7. Making the constituency a better place to live in, in terms of all the aspects above, so that there is a possibility of reverse migration.

8. In essence, the constituency should have sustainable development with a protected environment which will make the elected leader a friend, philosopher and guide of each and every family of the constituency.

I would also like to suggest some areas where the constituency development fund can be used. Members of Parliament are eligible for allocation of constituency development fund (MPLADS) of ₹5 crore every year. This fund can be used for important infrastructural activities, which will be beneficial to the citizens of the constituency. Some of the programmes which can be implemented through this fund could be:

1. Identifying the water bodies in the constituency that need desilting and opening of the inlet and outlet. Whenever there is rain, only the desilted tanks will be filled up and the level of the ground water in the region will increase. Linking up the water bodies in the constituency is also a possibility.

2. Education for girls needs the highest priority. Some of the major reasons why girls are not sent to school is the non-availability of toilets and the distance of the school from the village. There are

many schools with just a single room. MPs and MLAs can assist the existing school to improve infrastructure or start schools in the constituency with child-friendly infrastructure.

3. A survey of PHCs can be conducted to ensure that the centre is provided with doctors and minimum supporting staff along with equipment and medicines. Funds for tele-medicine connectivity between PHCs and the district hospital in the region can be allocated which will enable access to quality healthcare to the citizens.

4. For providing medical care to the remote areas of the constituency, provision of well-equipped mobile hospitals could be considered which will go to different villages of the constituency on specified dates, so that the patients can be treated in the village itself.

5. Development of state-of-the-art skills in welding, construction, repair and maintenance of electronic equipment will provide value-added employment to the youth. Special courses for the youth of the constituency can be organized for them to acquire skills in polytechnics or ITI located in the constituency or the district headquarters. This would be a great opportunity to create a global cadre of skilled people.

6. Organizing street plays in the constituency depicting the social evils such as dowry, corruption, female foeticide, gender inequality, child marriage and corruption can also be organized, so that the citizens of the constituency are made aware and facilitated to improve their societal characteristics. This will be a great opportunity to create a value-based system.

The message that I am trying to convey is that a democracy with developmental politics has to be the focus of our parliamentary system, since the nation is bigger than the political system.

WHAT WILL I BE REMEMBERED FOR?

Finally, I would like to ask every reader one question: what would you like to be remembered for? You have to evolve and shape your own life. You should write your goal down on a piece of paper. That page might just be a very important page in the book of human history. And you will be remembered for creating that page in the history of the nation—whether that is a page of invention, of innovation, of discovery, of creating societal change, of removing poverty, of fighting injustice or planning and executing a mission for energy independence. And I will be happy if you could mail me this page of yours at apj@ abdulkalam.com

The Environment Challenge

IT IS well known that throughout human history, four main sources of fuels have been used. There was wood in the ancient times, perhaps starting when fire was discovered, some one million years ago. The second major source was petroleum products, starting as late as the nineteenth century. The third source was nuclear, which came about as recent as fifty years ago. The fourth and newest source of energy are renewable resources like solar and wind. These have become commercially viable and technologically feasible in the last two decades.

Now, we are also talking of another important innovation in the energy sector—the fifth fuel. The fuel is energy efficiency. Various reports suggest that building energy efficiency is perhaps the most economically feasible and convenient way to 'generate' energy by actually saving it. Instead of advanced technology, it needs social awareness and incentives for industries and homes to go green. In India, like most developing nations, there is a great scope for this fifth source of energy. For instance, in distribution of power alone, the losses are over 40 per cent in many states. There is also immense scope for bringing about energy efficiency at household levels ranging from efficient use of cooking fuels to creating smart buildings which can save up to 50 per cent of the energy consumption.

To empower the growth of any nation, it is essential to evolve perspectives that will help realize the aim of energy independence. Energy independence has to be built on the foundation of innovative principles of environmental impact mitigation, selecting the right energy mix directly linked to sustainable economic growth and the use of fifth fuel, i.e., constantly improving energy efficiency in an integrated way.

GLOBAL ENVIRONMENT CHALLENGE

Today, the greatest challenge to the collective interest of humanity is the challenge of climate change due to the effect of anthropogenic greenhouse gas emissions. Globally, we are generating over thirty-six billion tonnes of CO_2 equivalent greenhouse gases annually into the atmosphere which is leading to increasing temperatures and increasing sea levels, endangering many low-altitude regions of the world.

In India, we need to preserve Sunderbans, the largest delta and mangrove forest in the world. Satellite imagery has shown that the sea level has risen in the area at a rate of 3.14 centimetres per year. This will adversely affect this area 20,000 square kilometres in size, marked by rich and rare bio-diversity and home to nearly five million people. Scientists say that the Sunderbans is south Asia's largest 'carbon sink'—it mops up carbon dioxide—and is an invaluable resource to help prevent global warming.

In order to reduce the effect of global warming, we need to launch a number of missions such as alternative energy generation systems and large scale tree plantation missions.

Our national action plan emphasizes eight national missions representing multi-pronged and long-term integrated strategy for achieving key goals in environmental impact mitigation. These missions are national solar mission, national mission for enhancement of energy efficiency, national mission for sustainable habitat, national water mission, national mission for Himalayan ecosystem, national mission for sustainable agriculture and national mission for strategic knowledge for climate change. In order to achieve a sustainable development path, these missions aim at protecting the vulnerable sections of the society, achieving national growth objectives.

ENERGY SECURITY VS ENERGY INDEPENDENCE

It is now widely understood that the climate of the globe as a whole is changing and we have to collectively work towards preserving a habitable planet earth.

Energy security means ensuring that our country can supply energy to all its citizens at affordable costs at all times using fossil fuels and other renewable energy mix. However, this must be considered as a transition strategy to eventually achieve energy independence. In the energy independent economy, there will be total or near total freedom from the use of fossil fuels such as coal, oil and gas leading to clean-green environment. Energy generation will occur from renewable energy sources such as wind, solar, hydro and nuclear energy and other forms of distributed modular energy generation options using alternate forms of energy. How to achieve it? That is where innovative solutions are needed.

ENERGY INDEPENDENCE BY 2030

We must be determined to achieve energy independence by the year 2030. For this, proper policy must be formulated and the missions have to be entrusted to the younger generation as public-private partnerships.

Energy Consumption Pattern in India

We have to critically look at the need for energy independence in the electric power generation sector. At present, we have an installed capacity of about 205,000 MW of electricity.

Forecasts of our energy requirements by 2030, when our population may touch 1.4 billion people, indicate that demand from the power sector will increase from the existing 205,000 MW to about 400,000 MW. This assumes an energy growth rate of 5 per cent per annum.

India has large potential for generating power through hydel resources and has a potential of 84,000 MW hydel power with 60 per cent plant load factor. Large scale solar energy farms of hundreds of megawatts capacity could contribute around 55,000 MW. Our nuclear scientists have an integrated energy policy with a target of generating 63,000 MW by 2030. On a conservative basis, I am sure that we will be able to generate 45,000 MW of power by 2030.

Another 45,000 MW of electrical power should come from wind energy. We are in a good state with respect to generation of wind energy.

Within the last decade, we have reached a capacity of generating over 11,000 MW through large scale wind farms. With this experience, it is possible to enhance our capacity to 45,000 MW by using low wind energy windmills by 2030.

Even though we will be building the gross capacity of 195,000 MW in the renewable energy sector, we have to build additional capacity to meet the challenges arising from volatile supply of renewable energy system. We have to also work on grid integration and de-centralized power supplies in widely dispersed remote areas. I consider that we may have to create 30 per cent additional capacity, that is around 60,000 MW, using modified thermal power plants having gasified coal and other resources like bio-mass and municipal waste. The most significant aspect of energy independence mission would be that the power generated through renewable energy technologies will be increased to nearly 65 per cent against the present 34 per cent.

For example, today India has 30,000 MW of captive power with the industry which can be fed by the private companies and used for national purposes for meeting volatile supply. Today, the problem is, this captive power is costly and environmentally unfriendly. To make it affordable with consistent environmental impact reduction, our scientists are working on an emulsification model which uses 50 per cent diesel and 50 per cent water in the diesel generating sets.

Prime electric power generation in India today accesses four basic energy sources: fossil fuels such as oil, natural gas and coal; hydroelectricity; nuclear power; and renewable energy sources such as bio-fuels, solar, biomass, wind and ocean. 89 per cent of input used for power generation today is indigenous, from coal (55 per cent), diesel and gas (11 per cent), hydroelectricity (21 per cent), nuclear power (2 per cent) and renewable (11 per cent). Solar energy segment contributes just 0.5 per cent of our energy production today.

According to a 2011 report by Bridge to India and GTM Research, India is facing a perfect storm of factors that will drive solar photovoltaic (PV) adoption at a 'furious pace over the next five years and beyond'. The falling prices of PV panels, mostly from China but also from the U.S., have coincided with the growing cost of grid power in India.

Government support and ample solar resources have also helped to increase solar adoption. With this background, we have the good news in solar power generation of one of our states in western India creating 654.8 MW of solar energy power within a short time and started feeding into the grid. Another state in the south aims to add 3,000 MW of solar power in three years' time. The reverse bidding process introduced by the Electricity Authority of India with the ceiling of rupees 15 per unit has brought in competition all of which is an advantage for the creation of clean green power. Now with increased competition, the state electricity boards are able to get the energy at an attractive price of rupees seven per unit. This may get further reduced when large scale installation and capacity addition takes place in a number of states and union territories. Such innovations should be multiplied and applied in all areas of energy production and management.

My analysis shows that only 11 per cent of electric power generation is dependent on oil and natural gas which is mostly imported at enormous cost. Only 1 per cent of oil is used every year for producing electricity. However, power generation to the extent of 10 per cent is dependent on high cost gas supplies. With the recent findings of oil and natural gas in different regions of the country, the cost effectiveness of these plants will further go up. Even though India has abundant quantities of coal, it is produced in regional locations with high ash content, affecting the thermal efficiency of our power plants, as well as increasing the environmental concerns. Keeping this in mind, Indian power sector has been constantly developing higher capacity power plants which has now reached 660 MW (a super critical unit). Also, there has been consistent improvement of plant load factor of thermal power stations and projects to deal with clean development mechanism. Very soon, we may go for ultra super critical technology. We have also accelerated the production of energy from the coal sector through much needed integrated gasification and combined cycle route.

My suggestions for India's energy future are the following:

Solar power panelled houses and street lights: India has approximately

200 million houses out of which 60 million houses do not have access to electricity. My suggestion is the necessity of a national policy to provide grid independent solar panel houses to these dwellings which can be extended to other 140 million houses gradually. Also the street lights can be provided on community based solar panels in villages, towns and cities. This will bring to India a vibrant solar panel industry right from innovative development, efficiency enhancement, production, distribution, marketing and maintenance of trouble free solar energy system as a business. This integrated business solution will bring down the cost of solar power generation and also distribution loss. The action of creating solar paneled houses and street lights will release nearly 50,000 to 60,000 MW of power for use by various sectors of the economy propelling national growth. It will also be useful for providing low cost electricity to other developing nations in the world.

Reducing distribution loss: We can reduce distribution loss substantially by introducing high voltage distribution system with appropriate modification of existing distribution system. This strategy is already prevalent in some of the distribution companies.

Captive power with industry: As I discussed earlier, India has 30,000 MW of captive power at present located in different industries. The suggestion is, we can increase this captive power in various forms to 60,000 MW (captive power generated by future industries) with a provision to feed into the grid unutilized captive generation capacity for meeting volatile supply of large scale renewable energy systems. All the captive power is powered by diesel fuel. By the new technology of emulsification which is an Indian innovation, 40 per cent fuel can be saved.

Research and development input: Academic institutions and R&D institutions both in public and private sector will work on the science and technology needed for energy independence as a prime research area for the next two decades.

Subsidizing electricity: Generating transmission and distribution institutions should not be loaded with any subsidy towards electricity. Whatever subsidy is required to be given for economically vulnerable sections of the society should be directly given by the government as is being proposed in respect of kerosene and diesel.

Formation of the National Energy Commission: This national agency will bring all the policy makers, planners both at the state and centre levels, ministries dealing with various forms of energy such as coal, petroleum and natural gas, MNES, irrigation and Ministry of Environment to ensure coordinated thrust and fast decision making for implementing the overall energy policy of the nation consistent with the demand for 10 per cent growth of the GDP.

In a democratic environment, people may have questions as to how these missions will bring a sustainable environment as time bound targets. Certainly it is a big challenge, but we must realize that when the economy grows, purchasing capacity grows and so does the efficiency of generating systems. By saving energy through modern technology, the cost will become affordable to the consumer and there will be very limited fear of revenue loss.

We may think some of this is impossible. But we need to look back at examples of success stories from our own recent history. Mahatma Gandhi's vision of independent India transformed India into a democracy. Dr C. Subramaniam's Agriculture Vision enabled India to realize the Green Revolution. Dr Varghese Kurien's Milk Vision led to India's White Revolution. Prof. Vikram Sarabhai's Space Vision enabled India to join the space club. Dr Homi Bhabha's Nuclear Vision led India to become a nuclear power.

Let us all learn to think positively and ambitiously and the aim of energy independence and clean and green energy solutions will not be impossible.

SECTION 5

Lectures

*A teacher's life lights
many lamps.*

1

SPEECH AT THE NATIONAL CONFERENCE ON VISION 2026, NEW DELHI, 26 NOVEMBER 2006

Sᴘᴇᴀᴋɪɴɢ ᴀʙᴏᴜᴛ science and making science accessible to all, especially children, is close to Dr Kalam's heart. Here he speaks about Prof. Yash Pal who has done just this. The speech was delivered at the inauguration of the National Conference on Vision 2026—Challenges in Science Communication in New Delhi on 26 November 2006, on the occasion of Prof. Yash Pal's eighty-first birthday.

PROF. YASH PAL AND SCIENCE

Prof. Yash Pal has made a substantial contribution to Indian science, science applications and science propagation. Whenever I see Prof. Yash Pal, I always see in front of me three events. The first one I remember is, when I was working with space scientists, periodically Prof. Yash Pal used to visit TERLS (Thumba Equatorial Rocket Launching Station), and give beautiful suggestions to protect the delicate payloads from the shock generated by the rocket during take-off and the flight sequence. The suggestions were useful and I used to telephone him to tell him how his suggestions totally worked during the integration of the sounding rocket payloads and flight. The second event took place in 1980, when I was busy with the SLV-3 launch at Sriharikota. Prof. Yash Pal was busy in setting up the Kytonn experiment, which is a tethered balloon for communication medium platforms. It had many technological innovations. This thought at that time was very new, today in many parts of the world it has become an operational system, particularly in the defence sector and hilly regions. The third event was when Prof. Yash Pal saw my team working on multiple tasks and suggested that I must build a chicken-mesh antenna for the SITE experiment. This development should compete with two more engineering groups in the country. He gave stringent specifications and demanded that the antenna should be very cost-effective, and should be built and delivered within three months' time. It was done. This chicken-mesh antenna was intended to receive the educational programme broadcast through the communication satellite for remote villages in India.

When he was director of the Space Application Centre, and later as secretary general for UNISPACE and the chairman of UGC and in whatever task he undertook, his mission was to empower the children and the youth, particularly the rural village folk, with proper education and skills. NCERT has prepared the national curriculum framework under Prof. Yash Pal's leadership and modified the CBSE syllabus for promoting creative education at all levels through the application of the 'learning by doing' concept. He is the most sought-after person at the children's science congress, and the children seek answers from him in large numbers. He has a unique way of answering the questions of the children by constantly interacting with them and making them understand the answer through the discussion process itself. It is a beautiful scene to watch.

Eighty years, what does it mean? Indeed, today, after completing eighty orbits around the sun, Prof. Yash Pal is entering into the eighty-first orbit, and there are many more orbits to come. The eighty beautiful years with his cheerful family is indeed God's blessing and I wish him and his family all the best on this occasion.

2

ADDRESS AT THE INAUGURAL SESSION OF THE PAN-AFRICAN PARLIAMENT, 16 SEPTEMBER 2004

INDIA AND PAN-AFRICAN NATIONS—PARTNERS IN DEVELOPMENT

Madam President and Honourable Members of the Pan-African Parliament.

I am honoured to have been called upon to participate in the opening ceremony of the second Pan-African Parliament Session of the African Union. I am delighted to extend my greetings and those of over one billion people of India to the members of this Pan-African Parliament which is the largest union of a group of countries who share similar and almost identical political social and economic environments. I consider this union, which unites about 3,000 distinct national communities speaking about thousand different languages as a harbinger of hope, not only for the members of African Union, but for the whole world. This is a great example of unity in diversity in action which has been the way of life in my country over five millennia.

FOCUS AFRICA

'Focus Africa' programme is one of the highest priority items for India. May I share with you my government's decision towards 'Focus Africa'.

My government has taken a special initiative for Africa, pledging $ 200 million in the form of credit line as part of the New Partnership for African Development (NEPAD) Scheme. My government has also announced a second scheme TEAM-9 initiative with a certain

173

number of African countries with an outlay of $ 500 million. These initiatives aim at the long-term economic development of certain African countries. Joint task teams have to be formed for mission-mode operation to derive maximum benefits in the shortest possible time.

Madam President and Hon'ble Members will agree with me that for India and the African nations, the common enemy is poverty and disease. We must launch technology missions to combat these enemies. As a first step we should embark on a connectivity mission among the nations—electronic connectivity and knowledge connectivity enabling economic connectivity of the region. For this, we propose a programme to connect all the fifty-three nations of the African Union by a satellite and fibre optic network. Apart from providing effective communication and connectivity among the nations, the same link will support tele-education, tele-medicine, e-governance, e-commerce, infotainment, resource mapping and meteorological services. This network will give rural connectivity to the entire Pan-African Union—an effective way to use technology to provide democratic access and empowerment.

Yesterday, I had a discussion with my prime minister. In honour of the Indo-Pan-African partnership, our government has decided to provide seamless and integrated satellite, fibre optics and wireless network connecting fifty-three African countries for tele-education, tele-medicine and e-services. This will connect five universities, fifty-three learning centres; ten super specialty hospitals and fifty-three patient-end locations in rural areas. This will cost about $50 million for installation, initial operation and maintenance for three years. It will be in position within the next three years and all the African nations participating in this network would be able to reap the full benefits. The Pan-African Parliament can form task teams for speedy and smooth implementation of the programme. We can jointly work together. An Indo-Pan-African joint team can make a comprehensive proposal and prepare a roadmap.

HEALTHCARE MISSION

Various parts of the world are getting affected by HIV/AIDS in addition to other communicable diseases. It is time that national and international agencies join together to mount a concerted programme in eliminating these dreaded diseases from planet earth. India has already ventured into the field of anti-AIDS vaccine. We are also mounting programmes to eradicate the new strains of other communicable diseases like TB and malaria. Certainly India and African countries can join together and quicken progress.

ENTREPRENEURSHIP AND EMPLOYMENT GENERATION

Based on our own experience, I would suggest that it is necessary to technologically upgrade small and medium industries for employment generation. In order to achieve this, there has to be an all-round improvement in technology and quality management, skill upgradation for existing and potential employees, and aggressive marketing. In addition, we need to make the youth seek entrepreneurship so that they can be employment generators rather than employment seekers.

CONCLUSION

I have been in this beautiful continent for the last one week. I have enjoyed its natural beauty. I have also gained a lot through sharing of ideas with many personalities. That inspired me to compose a poem. Let me read it out for you:

> The ocean connects us,
> The waves are our music.
>
> The sky connects us,
> The earth and sun give us life.
>
> Clouds connect us.
> Their impregnations give us rain.
>
> Everything in the universe connects us,
> Oh! human beings, why not you connect your hearts.

In Africa you have already entered into such a great mission towards unity of minds through this Pan-African Parliament. May you succeed in your endeavours.

May God bless you.

3

ADDRESS TO THE EUROPEAN
PARLIAMENT AT STRASBOURG, 24 APRIL 2007

DYNAMICS OF THE UNITY OF NATIONS

The confluence of civilizations is definitely possible.

I am delighted to be with the Honourable Members of European Parliament on the occasion of the golden jubilee year of the European Union. I was thinking, what thoughts can I share with you. India as a democratic nation has the experience of providing leadership to over one billion people with multi-language, multi-culture and multi-religious systems. I wish to share this experience with you.

EUROPEAN UNION FOR PEACE AND PROSPERITY

The European civilization has a unique place in human history. Its people were valiantly engaged in the adventure of exploring planet earth, resulting in the discovery of many ideas and systems. Europe has seen the birth of pioneers in science leading to technologies. Europe was the theatre of conflicts for hundreds of years among and between the nations, including the two world wars. Now, with this backdrop and dynamics, you have established the European Union with a vision for peace and prosperity for the entire region. The European Union has become an example of connectivity among nations, probably with no possibility of war, leading to lasting regional peace.

INTER-CONNECTEDNESS

Before I started out on my journey to Europe, I was thinking, why are Europe and India unique and natural partners? Do we share a common history and heritage, possibly in future, a common destiny? What I found was astonishing: the depth and vitality of our inter-connectedness, by language, by culture, by ancient beliefs, ideologies and the movement of people have stood the test of time. This has matured into a very strong bond through sustained trade and intellectually satisfying collaborations in many areas of science and technology.

UNITY IN DIVERSITY

India is a country which has, over the years, learnt to evolve and maintain a unique unity amongst diversity. Similarly, the greatest contribution of the European Union is that you have demonstrated to the world that it is possible to build a strong union of nations without compromising on national identities. It has become an inspirational model and an example to emulate for every region in the world. The European Union and India support a social form of economic development and encourage a model of growth with equity. Both are conscious of the need for growth with respect for the environment and make it sustainable for future generations. With this valuable experience of centuries behind India and the European Union, we can bring together a doctrine of global cooperation built over the foundation of regional collaborations and core competencies of nations.

With this background, I have brought from India a message, a message to start three important Indo-European missions which can contribute to global peace and prosperity based on India's experience and the dynamics of the European Union.

1. **Evolution of an Enlightened Society**—for evolving a citizen with value systems leading to prosperous and peaceful world.
2. **Leading to Energy Independence**—A three-dimensional approach to energy choices towards realizing a clean planet earth.

3. **World Knowledge Platform**—for synergizing the core competencies of the European Union and India in certain areas for providing solutions to critical issues like water, healthcare and capacity building.

TOWARDS A COHESIVE SOCIETY

When nations join together to build a cohesive society, it is necessary to ensure that the benefits of development encompass all sections of society. The world over, poverty, illiteracy, unemployment and deprivation are driving forward the forces of anger and violence. These forces link themselves to some earlier real or perceived historical enmities, tyrannies, injustice, inequities, ethnic issues and religious fundamentalism flowing into an outburst of extremism worldwide. Both India and the European Union have witnessed and are witnessing the unsavory acts of certain misguided sections of society. We have to jointly address ourselves to the root causes of such phenomena for finding lasting solutions for promoting peace.

RIGHTEOUSNESS IS THE BEGINNING

What we need is a carrier of eternal goodness and wholesomeness in human conduct, which is 'Righteousness'.

As we say in India:

Where there is righteousness in the heart
There is beauty in the character.
When there is beauty in the character,
There is harmony in the home.
When there is harmony in the home.
There is an order in the nation.
When there is order in the nation,
There is peace in the world.

This is true for the whole world. When we need peace in the world, we need order in the nation; we need harmony in the home, whether in Europe or in India or in any part of the world, the origin is righteousness in the heart. How do we evolve righteousness in the hearts of every citizen of the world?

I. Evolution of an Enlightened Society

With this spirit of righteousness in the heart, dear Honorable Members, I would like to put forth to this important gathering a methodology for evolving a happy, prosperous and peaceful society on our planet, which I call 'Evolution of the Enlightened Society'. I have shared these thoughts with many intellectuals in national and international spheres. How do we create such an enlightened society which will have three components (a) Education with value systems (b) Religion transforming into spirituality, and (c) Economic development for societal transformation? Let us discuss.

a. Education with Value Systems

We have seen that the seeds of peace in the world have their origin in the righteousness in the heart of every individual. Such righteous citizens lead to the evolution of enlightened societies. Education with value systems has to be so designed that the righteousness in the heart is developed in young minds. That should be the mission of education. The prime learning environment is five to seventeen years of age. This reminds me of an ancient Greek teacher's saying, 'Give me a child for seven years; afterwards, let God or devil take the child. They cannot change the child.' This indicates the power of great teachers and what they can inculcate in the young minds. Parents and teachers must inculcate moral leadership among children. It requires the ability to have insights into the uniqueness and the universality of the human consciousness. True education is the acquisition of enlightened feelings and enlightened powers to understand daily events and to understand the permanent truth linking man—to his environment, human and planetary.

While I was in college, I remember the lectures given by the highest authority of a Jesuit institution, Rev. Father Rector Kalathil of St. Joseph College, Tiruchirappalli, southern India. Every week on Monday, he would take a class for an hour. He used to talk about good human beings present and past and what makes a good human being. In this class he used to give lectures on personalities such as Buddha, Confucius, St. Augustine, Califa Omar, Mahatma Gandhi, Einstein, Abraham Lincoln and moral stories linked to our civilizational heritage. In the moral science class, Father Kalathil used to highlight the best aspects of how the great personalities have evolved as good human beings through parental care, teaching and companionship of great books. Even though these lessons were given to me in the 1950s during my college days, they inspire me even today. It is essential that in the schools and colleges, lectures are given by great teachers of the institution once in a week for one hour on civilizational heritage and derived value systems. This may be called 'moral science class' that will elevate young minds to love the country, to love other human beings and elevate them to higher planes. I have suggested this methodology to educationists in my country. The European Union may like to consider evolving a system that will enable a student to imbibe these fundamental traits for the benefit of all.

Now, let me take up the area that is transforming religion into a spiritual force. Many in the world believe it is a difficult mission. I would like to share an experience that I have witnessed which has convinced me that it is possible.

b. Religion Transforming into Spirituality: The Universal Mind

Religion has two components, theology and spirituality. Even though theology is unique to every religion, the spiritual component spreads the value to be inculcated by human beings for promoting a good human life and welfare of the society, while pursuing the material life. I would like to share an experience about how religion and science came together in a big mission.

It was during early 1960s; the founder of Indian Space Research programme, Prof. Vikram Sarabhai, with his team, had located a place technically most suited for space research after considering many alternatives. The place called, Thumba, in Kerala, was selected for space research as it was near the magnetic equator, ideally suited for ionospheric and electrojet research in the upper atmosphere. I was fortunate to work with Prof. Vikram Sarabhai for about eight years.

The major challenge for Prof. Sarabhai was to get the place in a specific area. As was normal, Prof. Vikram Sarabhai approached the Kerala government administrators first. After seeing the profile of the land and the sea coast, the view expressed was that thousands of fishing folk lived there, the place had the ancient St. Mary Magdalene Church, the Bishop's House and a school. Hence it would be very difficult to give this land, though they were willing to provide land in an alternative area. Similarly, the political system also opined that it would be a difficult situation due to the existence of important institutions and the concern for people who were to be relocated. However, there was a suggestion to approach the only person who could advise and help. That was the bishop, Rev. Father Peter Bernard Pereira. Prof. Sarabhai, approached the Bishop on a Saturday evening, I still remember. The meeting between the two turned out to be historical. Many of us witnessed the event. Rev. Father exclaimed, 'Oh Vikram, you are asking for my children's abode, my abode and God's abode. How is it possible?' Both had a unique quality that they could smile even in difficult situations. Rev. Father Pereira asked Prof. Sarabhai to come to church on Sunday morning at 9 Prof. Sarabhai went to the church again on Sunday with his team. At that time the prayer was progressing with recitation the Bible by Father Pereira. After the prayer was over, the Bishop invited Prof. Sarabhai to come to the dais. The Rev. Father introduced Prof. Sarabhai to the mass. 'Dear children, here is a scientist, Prof. Vikram Sarabhai. What do sciences do? All of us experience science. I am able to talk to you through the mike which is made possible by technology. The treatment of patients by doctors comes from medical sciences. Science through technology enhances the comfort and quality of human life. What do I do as a preacher? I pray for you, for your well being, for your peace. In short, what Vikram is doing and what I am doing are the same—both science and spirituality seek the Almighty's blessings for human prosperity in body and mind. Dear children, Prof. Vikram says he would build, within a year, near the sea-coast, alternative facilities to what we are having. Now dear children, can we give our abode, can we give my abode, can we give the God's abode for a great scientific mission?' There was a total silence, a pin-drop silence. Then all of them got up and said 'Amen' which made the whole church reverberate.

That was the church where we had our design centre, where we started rocket assembly and the bishop's house was our scientists' working place. Later, the Thumba Equatorial Rocket Launching Station (TERLS) led to the establishment of the Vikram Sarabhai Space Centre (VSSC) and the space activities transformed into multiple space centres throughout the country. Now this church has become an important centre of learning, where thousands of people learn about the dynamic history of the space programme of India and the great minds of a scientist and spiritual leader. Of course, the Thumba citizens got well-equipped facilities, a worshipping place and an educational centre in an alternate place at the right time.

When I think of this event, I can see how enlightened spiritual and scientific leaders can converge towards giving reverence to human life. Of course, the birth of TERLS, and then VSSC, gave the country the capability for launch vehicles, spacecraft and space applications that have accelerated social and economic development in India to unprecedented levels.

Today, among us, Prof. Vikram Sarabhai is not there, Rev. Peter Bernard Pereira is not there, but those who are responsible for creating and making flowers blossom will themselves be a different kind of flower as described in the Bhagavad Gita: 'See the flower, how generously it distributes perfume and honey. It gives to all, gives freely of its love. When its work is done, it falls away quietly. Try to be like the flower, unassuming despite all its qualities.' What a beautiful message to humanity on the purpose of life reflecting the spiritual component. Can we bridge the spiritual component of the religions to bring peace to nations and to the world?

I would like to recall one incident which commonly occurs in many parts of my country. I have witnessed this event when I was a young boy about ten years old. In our house, I used to periodically see three different unique personalities meet. Pakshi Lakshmana Shastrigal, who was the head priest of the famous Rameswaram temple and a vedic scholar, Rev. Father Bodal, who built the first church on Rameswaram Island and my father who was an imam in the mosque. All three of them used to sit and discuss the island's problems and find solutions to them. In addition, they built several religious connectivities with compassion. These connectivities quietly spread to others in the island like the fragrance from flowers. This sight always comes to my mind whenever I discuss with people the dialogue of religions. India has had this advantage of integration of minds for thousands of years. Throughout the world, the need to have a frank dialogue among cultures, religions and civilizations is felt now more than ever.

These two instances that I have narrated give me confidence that religions definitely can be bridged through spiritual components. Whenever I meet the young and the inexperienced in my country, I narrate these two experiences. Many in my country and the world over may have such experiences. We have to spread such 'glad tidings' to every part of the world.

Now, let us discuss the third important component of an enlightened society which is to achieve economic development for societal transformation. Let me take my country India as an example, it may be true for many parts of the world.

c. Economic Development for Societal Transformation

The Indian economy is in an ascent phase. There is considerable growth in the manufacturing and service sectors. We have a mission of spreading this economic growth throughout the country, including the rural sector. Nearly 220 million people have to be uplifted by upgrading their quality of life in both rural and urban areas. Even though the GDP indicates our economic growth, people's participation is essential for achieving the required targets. It is essential to ensure that the citizens are empowered with a good quality of life encompassing nutritious food, good habitat, clean environment, affordable healthcare, quality education and productive employment, integrated with our value systems which have been drawn from our civilizational heritage leading to the comprehensive development of the nation that will bring smiles to one billion people. These are indicators for the growth of the National Prosperity Index. To achieve that growth rate, we have identified five areas where India has a core competence for integrated action: (1) Agriculture and food processing (2) Education and healthcare (3) Information and communication technology (4) Infrastructure development such as power, transportation, communication and including Providing Urban Amenities in Rural Areas (PURA) and (5) Self reliance in critical technologies. We propose to realize the vision of transforming India into a developed nation before 2020 by energizing and igniting the minds of all the 540 million youth of the nation.

So far, we have discussed the three-dimensional approach of providing value-based education, religion transforming into spiritual force and economic development for societal transformation leading to the evolution of an enlightened society. This integrated three-dimensional methodology of evolution of enlightened society will pave the way for peaceful, prosperous, happy nations and thereby a world free from extremisms and further seeds of extremism.

Let me now discuss the second mission: 'Leading to Energy Independence'.

II. Leading to Energy Independence

When we analyse the critical problems facing planet earth today, two important issues come to our minds. First one is the continuous depletion of fossil-material-derived oil, gas and coal reserves as predicted by World Energy Forum. The second one is the continuous degradation of the environment, primarily due to extensive use of fossil materials for generating energy. The solution to these problems can be found through energy independence, which I have presented to my country. It may be applicable to many nations.

Energy Independence in India—A Perspective: India has 17 per cent of the world's population, but only about 0.8 per cent of the world's known oil and natural gas resources. Based on the progress visualized for the nation during the next two decades, the power-generating capacity has to increase to 400,000 MW by the year 2030 from the current

130,000 MW in India. This takes into consideration energy economies planned and the design and production of energy-efficient equipment and systems. Energy independence has to be achieved through three different sources, namely, renewable energy (solar, wind and hydro power), electrical power from nuclear energy, and bio-fuel for the transportation sector. Energy independence throws very important technological challenges to the world. The solar cell efficiency has to increase from the present 20 per cent to 55 per cent through intensified research on CNT (Carbon Nano Tube)-based solar cells. For thorium reactors, as it is known, thorium is a non-fissile material. It has to be converted into a fissile material using Fast Breeder Technology. In the bio-fuel area, the challenge is bio-fuel plantation for higher yield, esterification technologies for the higher output and the modification to automobile power plants. These three research areas definitely need intensive cooperation between the Europian Union and India. I would suggest setting up of an 'Indo-EU Renewable Energy Development programme' for taking up advanced R&D in all forms of renewable energy leading to the availability of commercial class large-scale power plants within the next decade.

Let us now discuss the third mission, called the World Knowledge Platform.

III. World Knowledge Platform

With the Indian experiences of two successful international cooperative ventures from concept to realization and marketing, I would suggest the evolution of a World Knowledge Platform for bringing together the core competence of multiple nations of the EU and India in science and technology leading to the development of unique systems for global applications.

The 'World Knowledge Platform' will enable the joint design, development, cost-effective production and marketing of knowledge products, systems and services in various domains based on the core competence of partner nations to international market. The World Knowledge Platform will be a meeting place for science, technology, industry, management and marketing.

Missions of the World Knowledge Platform: The convergence of bio, nano and IT technologies is expected to touch every area of concern to the humanity. It will take up the missions in some of the areas discussed further which are of utmost urgency to all of us to make our world a safe, sustainable, peaceful and prosperous place to live in.

1. **Water:** The desalination of sea water using solar energy; the channelization, networking of rivers cost-effective, safe drinking water.

2. **Healthcare:** Diagnosis; drug delivery system; development and production of vaccines for HIV/TB, malaria and cardiac diseases; detection and cure of diabetes.

3. **Agriculture and food processing:** Increased production of food grain in an environment of reduced land, reduced water and reduced manpower; preservation of food; food processing; cost-effective storage and distribution.

4. **Knowledge products:** Hardware, software and networking and storage products, including handheld micro- and nano- electronic devices.

5. **Transportation systems:** Fossil fuel-free transportation systems using renewable energies, safety systems, hardware and embedded software integration.

6. **Habitat:** Energy-efficient, water-efficient, pollution-free habitats.

7. **Disaster prediction and management:** Earthquake forecasting, assessing in advance the quantum of rain for particular cloud conditions.

8. **Capacity building:** Quality human resource development for all the above areas including the development of personnel with world-class skills.

The European Union represents a wealth of scientific potential with a rich culture of research. India has emerged as a leading country with its demonstrated scientific and technological potential in many societal missions and is now on the growth path. The combined strengths of the nations can be utilized for the mutual advantage of both India and the EU by joining together as partners in creating the World Knowledge Platform.

CONCLUSION

Honourable Members of European Parliament, as we have seen, there is a visible common thread of our dreams and problems. When I am with you, I have a feeling that there are beautiful solutions from beautiful minds. Beautiful minds generate creativity. This is the common heritage of both India and Europe. Dear Honourable Members of the European Union, I have presented three missions: (a) Evolution of Enlightened Society, (b) Leading to Energy Independence (c) Creating World Knowledge Platform. These Indo-EU missions will definitely reinforce our strategic partnership further and become the foundation for making the change in the life of 1.5 billion people, ultimately leading to the confluence of civilizations.

For meeting the challenges of these missions, we can draw the inspiration from the saying of Maharishi Patanjali, about 2,500 years ago: 'When you are inspired by some great purpose, some extraordinary project, all your thoughts break their bounds. Your mind transcends limitations, your consciousness expands in every direction, and you find yourself in a new, great and wonderful world. Dormant forces, faculties and talents come alive, and you discover yourself to be a greater person by far than you ever dreamt yourself to be.

4

ADDRESS AT THE NATIONAL ASSEMBLY, PHILIPPINES, 8 FEBRUARY 2006

NATIONAL MISSIONS FOR PROSPERITY

Dear friends, let me convey my greetings of one billion people of my country to all the Honourable Members of European Union and through you to all the citizens of European Union countries.

May God bless you.

It is a great honour that you have bestowed on the government and people of India, and indeed a delight for me, to address this National Assembly of on ancient and great nation. I am deeply conscious that your country is at a crucial turning point in its history. As you enter into a globalized world economy with its opportunities and crisis cycles, I know that you are looking forward with anxiety, as most countries of the world do at present, to what might appear as an uncertain future. I can assure you that the rich civilizational heritage and value systems you have will stand your nation and people in good stead as you move forward into the future. Same is the case with us. I assure you that we in India share your feelings and thoughts as close friends. We have also passed through similar times, not just in recent history, but also over many centuries of our existence. As ancient civilizations, we both are endowed with a wide variety of cultural and ethnic diversity.

WORKING TOGETHER

I am thankful for the privilege of sharing with you and the people of Philippines whom you represent, our experience in our efforts to develop the nation socially and economically over the last fifty years. I do so in a spirit of understanding that we may learn from each other and strengthen our resolve to move our nations ahead to greater prosperity, happiness and freedom from insecurity in the years ahead. Both our nations are free, independent states in an increasingly complex and interdependent world where the values of friendship and mutual assistance are of paramount importance.

INDO-PHILIPPINES FRIENDSHIP

Throughout recorded history, India has always been a friend of all nations and we are happy to be counted among the friends of Philippines. We have never at any time in our past invaded other countries or used destructive force to achieve any end. The hallmark of India throughout the ages has been 'All places are our native places and all our relatives'. This is deeply ingrained in the social and political life of India for thousands of years. For promoting peace we need development and that too all-round development. For achieving this aim India has a roadmap, particularly to develop the 600,000 villages where 70 per cent of our population resides. Our urban areas have already reached a stage of rapid growth and development. For reaching our villages with equal rapidity, it is planned to be achieved through a rural development programme called Providing Urban Amenities in Rural Areas (PURA).

ECONOMIC CONNECTIVITY FOR PURA

Providing Urban Amenities in Rural Areas (PURA) consisting of four connectivities: physical, electronic, knowledge and thereby leading to economic connectivity to enhance the prosperity of clusters of villages in rural areas. The economic connectivity will generate a market and the production establishments for servicing the market. PURA has all the dimensions to become a business enterprise which has global dimensions but is operating in every nook and corner of our country.

PURA entrepreneurs have to have the skill for evolving a business plan with banks and also create infrastructural support such as educational institutions, health centres and small-scale industries, transportation services, tele-education, tele-medicine, e-governance services in the region integrating with the governmental rural development schemes such as road, communication and transport and also with national and global markets to sell products and services.

PURA MODEL

Depending upon the region and the state of present development, PURA can be classified into three different categories, namely, Type A, Type B and Type C PURA clusters. The characteristics features of these types are given below:

The Type A Cluster is situated close to an urban area and has minimal road connectivity, limited infrastructure, limited support—for instance a school, or a primary health centre. Type B Cluster is situated closer to an urban area but has sparsely spread infrastructure and no connectivity, the Type C Cluster is located in the far interior with no infrastructure, no connectivity and no basic amenities. In addition to these are the coastal PURAs and the hill PURAs.

CRITERIA FOR PURA CLUSTERS

A Type A Cluster may have a population of 30,000 to 1,00,000 in about ten to fifteen villages with adequate land for a four-lane circular road, without obstacles such as canals, railway tracks or power lines, ensuring minimum displacement of people, and preferably falls within the district jurisdiction. Similar criteria need to be worked out for B and C clusters.

PURA ENTERPRISE

The small and medium industry enterprises in India have experience in managing the small- and medium-scale industries of different types in various regions. This sector is widespread in the country and is a promising candidate for taking leadership in managing PURA complexes in an integrated way. Also, major businesses in India with widespread rural services have experience in maintaining large rural-urban networks. PURA enterprises can undertake management of schools, healthcare units, vocational training centres, chilling plants, silos and building a market, building of local industrial/information and communication technology parks, environment-friendly manufacturing units, tourism services, banking systems and the regional business or industrial units. A new management style has to emerge for managing such PURA enterprises. This new PURA enterprise needs partnership from banks, educational institutions, the government and private entrepreneurs. The management system should have the flexibility to be competitive and the country has to experiment several models depending on local needs. Now I would like to discuss some of the operational PURAs in India.

Periyar PURA (Tamil Nadu): I inaugurated the Periyar PURA complex, pioneered by Periyar Maniammai College of Technology for Women, Vallam, Thanjavur a year ago. I thought of sharing with you the developmental concept of a cluster of over sixty-five villages near Vallam in the Thanjavur district of Tamil Nadu that involves a population of 3 lakh. This PURA complex has all the three connectivities—physical, electronic and knowledge—leading to economic connectivity. The centre of activity emanates from the women's engineering college that provides the electronic and knowledge connectivity. Periyar PURA has healthcare centres, primary-to post-graduate-level education and vocational training centres. This has resulted in large-scale employment generation and the creation of a number of entrepreneurs with the active support of 850 self-help groups. Two hundreds acres of wasteland has been developed into cultivable land with innovative water-management schemes such as contour ponds and watersheds for storing water and irrigating fields. All the villagers are busy in cultivation, planting Jatropha, herbal and medicinal plants, power generation using bio-mass, food processing and, above all, running marketing centres.

This model has emanated independent of any government initiative. Committed leadership has been provided by the engineering institution. Recently, five of the Periyar PURA villages were connected through WiMAX wireless technology with the Periyar PURA Nodal centre. It provides sustainable economic development in that region. This gives me the confidence that PURA is a realizable proposition and this movement can be multiplied by thousands of entrepreneurs, educational administrators, small-scale industrialists and bankers with the support of government agencies.

Loni PURA, Model (Maharashtra): Recently, I visited a place called Loni in Maharashtra where a participative model of integrated rural development has come up among forty-four villages with a population of eighty thousand. The Loni PURA model has been pioneered by the Pravara Medical Trust. It is improving the productivity of rural people through improved quality of life with healthcare, education and employment. The concept is people-centric development for social transformation. The thrust area of development has been on comprehensive medicare, particularly for women and children, need-based health education and e-connectivity to the farmers. The complex has created twenty-seven educational and vocational institutions consisting of schools, colleges, polytechnic and ITI including medical and engineering colleges. They have created sugar factories, biogas plants, chemical plants and power projects. They have large number of self-help groups for providing low-interest loans for the weaker sections in the society. Due to the co-operative effort of the people, literacy in these villages has gone up from 63 per cent to 83 per cent, the birth rate has come down, infant mortality rate has decreased to 35, per 1,000 from 70 per 1,000 and the standard of living of the people has gone up by over 20 per cent compared to other villages in the neighbouring areas.

Chitrakoot PURA (Madhya Pradesh) : Recently I visited Chitrakoot in Madhya Pradesh, where I met Shri Nana Deshmukhji—aged ninety—and his team members belonging to Deendayal Research Institute (DRI). DRI is a unique institution developing and implementing a village development model which is most suited for India.

The DRI understands that people's power is more potent, stable and enduring than political power. By becoming one with the oppressed and the depressed, one gains the acumen of administration and governance. Social advancement and prosperity are possible only by injecting the spirit of self-reliance and excellence in the younger generation. Using this principle, the DRI has plans to develop 100 clusters of villages having approximately five villages each around Chitrakoot. They have already developed eighty villages in sixteen clusters consisting of about 50,000 people.

I witnessed one of the villages called Patni where the institute has promoted sustainable development based on indigenous and traditional technology, knowledge systems and local talents. The research work by the institute through field studies facilitates the development of replicable and tangible models for achieving self-reliance in villages. The programme aims at income generation through value addition, innovative agricultural practices, inculcating scientific temper among villagers, improvement of health and hygiene, striving towards 100 per cent literacy. As a part of integrated rural development, the villagers are practising water harvesting and effectively use it for the cultivation of food grains, medicinal and aromatic plants and horticulture. Apart from all these development activities, the institute is facilitating a cohesive, conflict-free society. As a result of this, I understand that the eighty villages around Chitrakoot are almost litigation free. The villagers have unanimously decided that no dispute will find its way to court. The differences will be sorted out amicably in the village itself. The reason given by Nana Deshmukhji is that if the people fight among each other they have no time for development. They can neither develop themselves nor the community. This message has been understood by society and they have decided not to fight. All these have been accomplished through DRIs 'samaj shilpi dampati' (a graduate married couple) a new concept of counseling and intervention promoted by the DRI. It was a great joy for me to lunch with Patni village citizens. A new road connecting multiple villages in the Chitrakoot area is taking shape. In the same Chitrakoot environment there is another social organization called the Shri Sadguru Seva Sangh Trust which is carrying out a number of social activities including the running of a quality eye-care centre. In a rural environment, I find a revolution is taking place due to the committed leadership to remove the human pain.

Byrraju PURA: Recently, on 9 January 2006, I visited Bhimavaram in Andhra Pradesh where I saw the Byrraju PURA set up by the Byrraju Foundation (Andhra Pradesh). This foundation has undertaken the mission of establishing thirty-two Ashwini centres benefiting 116 villages with a population of around 500,000 people. It has provided electronic connectivity and knowledge connectivity. It has skill-enabled and knowledge-enabled citizens in multiple areas and created 3,000 jobs with a minimum earning of Rs. 3,000 per month; this is three times that of their earlier earning potential. They have created a Gram IT BPO which has brought 10 per cent reverse migration from Hyderabad to Bhimavaram—from the city to the village). I would suggest the other industry captains to come forward with such PURAs with physical connectivity, electronic connectivity and knowledge connectivity leading to large-scale employment and wealth generation in the region. This will enable emigration from cities to rural areas as I have noticed in Bhimavaram.

This foundation has also brought an emergency medical service to the people of five districts in Andhra Pradesh in association with the Emergency Management and Research Institute. When a person dials 108, a toll-free number, from any telephone, an Advanced Life Support System ambulance reaches promptly. They have saved more than 1,000 lives. The service has been extended to two more districts. International Disaster Management Agencies can take note of this experience for propagating such type of services in different countries.

Now I would like to discuss some of the areas like healthcare, renewable energy, deep-sea fishing, harnessing geo-thermal energy, bio-fuel plantations and earthquake prediction which are of interest to both our countries.

HEALTHCARE

The Indian healthcare community is giving highest priority to the treatment of HIV/AIDS and accelerating the development of effective anti-vaccine for certain types of HIV before 2007 by networking with national and international institutions working in this area. They are also integrating the research efforts of malaria, typhoid and diarrhoeal disorders for facilitating a development of the combination vaccine by 2007. Healthcare personnel, doctors, psychologists, researchers, pharmacologists, economists and environmentalists should all work together coherently towards the mission of providing good health to all citizens of India and make the nation near disease free. I would invite Philippines to become a partner in these programmes.

RENEWABLE ENERGY

On 17 January 2006, I visited the Kaylapara village on Sagar Island. There I saw the photovoltaic solar power plant of 120 KW capacity established by the West Bengal Renewable Energy Development Agency. At present, this is the largest off GRID solar power plant in the country. This power plant, along with many smaller power plants, is providing six hours of electrical energy to thirty-three villages of Sagar Island. I met children who were studying in Sagar Island using the energy generated by solar power plant. Apart from providing electricity for household purposes, a cold chain has been set up for storing and preserving agro-foods and milk produced in the village, which gives value-added revenue to the village community. This scheme is being replicated in many villages in the country. Since Philippines has more than seven thousand islands, I would suggest that such solar-power-based electrical systems be considered for implementation by the Philippines government.

DEEP-SEA FISHING, FISH PROCESSING AND MARKETING OF SEA FOOD PRODUCTS

When I visited Iceland in June 2005, I studied their economy; their highest per capita income comes from the fishing industry. Hence I took interest to study the fishing industry in Iceland. Even though they have a vast sea all around their territory, they have 'sea area silence'— during a particular period, no fishing boats are allowed to catch fish. This allows sufficient grown-up fish catch for the fishermen during rest of the period. Also, the sea zones are allotted to the fishermen based on satellite fish-school data. They have satellite surveillance and land communication to safeguard their economic zones, so that other countries do not enter for fishing. But the most important thing I would like to convey is their success in deep sea fishing. I visited one of the very big fish trawlers which has 200 tons fish processing capacity and 1,800 tons storage capacity. The deep sea fishing, fish processing, packaging and marketing—all these aspects take place in the middle of the sea. It gives a new dimension to the whole fishing industry. In India we are in the process of setting up deep sea fishing, processing and marketing in the Andaman and Nicobar Islands and some of the coastal regions. The Philippines government can study this model and consider setting up a deep sea fishing industry. India can help in locating deep sea fishing zones through the Indian Space Research Organisation (ISRO) by using satellites. This will enable the fishing community of Philippines to increase their per capita income substantially.

GEO-THERMAL ENERGY

Iceland is one of the world leaders in the field of geo-thermal energy. I visited one such plant which generates 90 MW, which also supplies heated water to the capital city Reykjavik. They are planning to build a 120 MW plant in the next phase. Iceland has plans to further intensify the development of this source of clean energy. Since Philippines also experiences volcanic eruptions, the availability of hot springs is a possibility. I would suggest that resource mapping be done and, if there are prospective springs, the Philippines government can consider creating geo-thermal energy plants for use on different islands.

BIO-FUEL GENERATION

In India, to supplement fossil fuel energy, we have undertaken large-scale plantation of Jatropha on both government and private land. The government has decided to permit the mixing of 10 per cent bio-fuel with diesel. The Indian Railways is using 100 per cent bio-fuel for running heavy vehicles like trucks, cranes, forklifts, jeeps and tractors. This has opened up new opportunities for employment and wealth generation. We have nearly 63 million hectares of wasteland available in the country, out of which 33 million hectares have been allotted for tree plantation. Certain multi-purpose trees such as Jatropha can grow well in wasteland with very little input. Once grown, the crop has a life of fifty years. Fruiting can take place in this plant in less than two years.

It yields oil seeds up to five tonnes per hectares per year and produces two tonnes of bio-diesel. Bio-diesel plants grown in 11 million hectares of land can yield a revenue of approximately $4 billion a year and provide employment to over twelve million people both for plantation and running of the extraction plants. This is a sustainable development process leading to large-scale employment of rural manpower. Five states in India have actively taken up this programme in a mission mode and Tamil Nadu and the Anand Agricultural University have generated expertise from the plantation of Jatropha to the extraction of bio-fuel through esterification. From the data available I find over 50 per cent of the land area of three lakh square kilometres of Philippines remains unused. India and Philippines can definitely work together to make productive use of this land for cultivating Jatropha and converting it into bio-fuel. This will lead to energy security to a certain extent.

EARTHQUAKE PREDICTION

In many places in our planet, we experience severe earthquakes resulting in the loss of life, the loss of wealth and, in some cases, the destruction of decades of progress made by the country and its valuable civilizational heritage. India has earthquake problems periodically in certain regions. Recently, in our state of Jammu and Kashmir and the neighbouring country, there was an earthquake. US, Japan, Turkey, Iran, Philippines and many other countries also suffer due to earthquakes. It is essential to forecast earthquakes using multiple parameters such as pre-shock conditions, electromagnetic phenomena prior to final rupture and atmospheric/ionospheric anomalies. India is taking up a time-bound programme for earthquake prediction. I would invite Philippine scientists to participate in the programme.

CONCLUSION: EMPOWERMENT

When a child is empowered by the parents at various phases of growth, the child gets transformed into a responsible citizen. When a teacher is empowered with knowledge and experience, good young human beings with value systems emerge. When an individual or a team is empowered with technology, transformation to higher potential for achievement is assured. When a leader of any village empowers his or her people, leaders are born who can change the nation in multiple areas. When women are empowered, a society with stability is assured. When the political leaders of the nation empower the people through visionary policies, the prosperity of the nation is certain. When religions are empowered and become spiritual forces, peace and happiness will blossom. Empowerment of the various layers of the management structure is indeed the best instrument to maximize the performance of a given fund to the developmental tasks. I am sure that the empowered people of Philippines, armed with knowledge and technology, will definitely lead to the prosperity, happiness and peace of the nation.

My best wishes to the members of this august Assembly in their mission of making Philippines an empowered, progressive nation of Asia.

5

THANKS-GIVING ADDRESS TO THE NATION, 24 JULY 2007

FIVE EVENTFUL YEARS

When you wish upon a star,
Makes no difference who you are
Anything your heart desires
Will come to you.

Friends, I am delighted to address you all, in the country and those living abroad, after working with you and completing five beautiful and eventful years in Rashtrapati Bhavan. Today, it is indeed a thanks-giving occasion. I would like to narrate how I enjoyed every minute of my tenure enriched by the wonderful association with each one of you, hailing from different walks of life, be it politics, science and technology, academics, arts, literature, business, judiciary, administration, local bodies, farming, home makers, special children, media and, above all, the youth and student community who are the future wealth of our country. During my interaction at Rashtrapati Bhavan in Delhi and at every state and union territory as well as through my online interactions, I have many unique experiences to share with you, which signify the following important messages:

1. Accelerate development;
2. Empower villages;
3. Mobilize rural core competence for competitiveness;
4. Seed to food: backbone for agricultural growth;
5. Defeat problems and succeed;

6. Overcome problems through partnership;
7. Courage in combating calamities;
8. Connectivity for societal transformation;
9. Defending the nation;
10. Youth movement for Developed India 2020.

Now let me share with you each of the messages.

ACCELERATE DEVELOPMENT

While there were many significant events during my tenure, a question from a little girl, Anukriti, of Sri Sathya Sai Jagriti Vidya Mandir School, of Darwa village from Haryana, during a children's visit to Rashtrapati Bhavan on 22 May 2006, rings in my mind ever after.

Anukriti asked me, 'Why can India not become a developed nation before the year 2020?' I appreciated the question and assured her that that her dream would be taken to the highest institution of the nation and we would work for it to be achieved before 2020. This question reflects how the desire to live in developed India has entered into the minds of the youth. The same feelings are echoed by over one and a half million youth whom I have met so far and who represent the dream of the 540 million youth of the nation. The aspirations of the young to live in a prosperous, safe and proud India should be the guiding factor in whatever profession we contribute.

EMPOWER VILLAGES

Friends, I recall my visit to Nagaland on 26 October 2002, soon after assuming office as President. It was a unique experience for me at Khuzama village to meet tribal village council members and discuss with them the village progress and the dream of village citizens. I was very happy to see the empowered village council functioning with financial powers and taking decisions. I saw a prosperous village with fruits and vegetables production. However, there is a need for providing physical connectivity in Nagaland through quality roads for enabling faster movement of products from villages to the market. That meeting gave me a powerful message about the transformation which can take place in the 600,000 villages of India if all the villages are empowered to deal with their development and are well connected among themselves and with urban societies.

MOBILIZING RURAL CORE COMPETENCE FOR COMPETITIVENESS

Now I would like to talk about the initiative of Periyar Maniammai College of Technology for Women, Vallam, Thanjavur, of Providing Urban Amenities in Rural Areas (PURA) complex involving sixty-five villages with a population of 300,000. This includes the provision of three connectivities—social, electronic and knowledge—leading to economic connectivity. Periyar PURA has healthcare centres, primary to post graduate-level education and vocational training centres. This has resulted in large-scale employment generation and the creation of number of entrepreneurs with the active support of 1,000 self-help groups. Two hundred acres of waste land has been developed into cultivable land. The villagers are busy in cultivation, planting Jatropha, herbal and medicinal plants, power generation using bio-mass, food processing, and, above all, running marketing centres. It provides a sustainable economic development model for the whole region.

During the last eight months, people of the Periyar PURA villages, technologically supported by the Periyar Maniammai College of Engineering for Women, have worked with experts from Japan External Trade Organisation (JETRO) on various products, for which core competence and raw material are available in the Thanjavur district. They developed internationally competitive prototypes for fifty-five lifestyle products with the support of JETRO specialists and feedback from exhibitions at Delhi and Tokyo. This co-operative venture has enhanced the innovative ability of the people of all the sixty-five villages, enabling them to develop and produce internationally acceptable products. I have seen similar types of PURAs being established in many states. The whole country needs 7,000 PURAs bridging the rural–urban divide.

SEED TO FOOD: BACKBONE FOR AGRICULTURAL GROWTH

Let me now share with you the enriching experience I had while meeting more than 6,000 farmers from different states and union territories visiting Rashtrapati Bhavan. They evinced keen interest in the Mughal Gardens, the Herbal Gardens, the Spiritual Garden, the Musical Garden, the Bio-diesel Garden and the Nutrition Garden and interacted with horticultural specialists. Recently, during my address to the agricultural scientists while participating in a national symposium 'Agriculture Cannot Wait', I summarized the many practical suggestions given by farmers. We have to double the agricultural production with reduced land, reduced water resources and reduced manpower and improve the economic conditions of the nation through the principle of 'Seed to Food' since agriculture is the backbone of the nation. We should empower the farmers to protect and nurture fertile land for a second Green Revolution. Meeting the scientists and the farmers has given me the confidence that the nation is poised to increase the agricultural GDP growth by atleast 4 per cent per annum through the partnership of farmers and agricultural scientists and industries, particularly for value addition.

DEFEAT THE PROBLEMS AND SUCCEED

On the evening of 24 February 2007, in Coimbatore, I had a very beautiful experience. As I got ready to meet the first person out of twenty appointments, a person in a wheelchair entered the room. He was in his fifties. He had a broad smile; unfortunately he had no hands and legs. His radiant face was revealing his happy state of mind. He introduced himself as Vidwan Coimbatore S.R. Krishna Murthy. I greeted him and asked him how this had happened. He smilingly said that it was from birth. He thanked God, his parents, teachers and many others for giving him confidence, training and help. I asked him what I could do for him. He said, 'I don't need anything from you. I would like to sing in front of you.' I readily agreed. He melodiously sang Saint Thyagraja's 'pancha ratna kriti entharo mahanubavulu' in

Sriragam, giving me a glimpse of his talent. I was quite touched. What is the message? Despite being physically challenged, the latent talent of music could blossom in this person with his positive attitude and perseverance, encouraged by parents, teachers, academics and rasikas. Now he wants to give, give and give his art to inspire others. Of course, by his merit of music, in July 2007, he performed in the Rashtrapati Bhavan art theatre.

OVERCOME THE IMPACT OF DISASTER THROUGH PARTNERSHIP

I had the opportunity to experience the indomitable spirit of the people and children of Jammu and Kashmir even as they were just recovering from the devastating earthquake in 2005. I visited Urusa village on 26 November 2005 which had been adopted by the Western Air Command, Air Force, for providing relief and medical aid to the residents of that area. When I went there, I found that the school building had been severely damaged. I met all the schoolchildren and the village citizens of Urusa. The villagers apprised me of their losses and had all praise for the Army and the Air Force for their role in rescue and relief operations along with the state government. I appreciate the courage of the people of Urusa in defeating their problems. They have actually become the master of the problem rather than allowing problems to become their master. Despite the severe loss due to the earthquake, the children and the members of the village participated in the relief operation with the Armed Forces bravely and were smiling when I went to meet them. They interacted with me and said that the school was functional in temporary tents. Here, I also witnessed the participation of the acting chief justice of Jammu and Kashmir along with state government authorities in on-the-spot settlement of relief grants to be provided to the victims whose houses had been damaged in the earthquake. I have experienced many such acts of courage from our citizens when faced with severe challenges.

COURAGE IN COMBATING CALAMITIES

In 2005, I met the tribal council leaders, students and children of Chuckchucha village during my visit to the Car Nicobar Islands. While various reconstruction and rehabilitation activities were in progress, during the discussions with the members of tribal council, I realized a unique trait of the Car Nicobar islanders. Even though there were many human losses due to the tsunami of 26 Dec 2004, the tribal islanders had taken possession of affected victims as their children and there was nothing like an orphanage in the Car Nicobar Islands. Touched by their courage, I composed few verses called 'Sea Waves' which reads as follows:

> We are the children of sea waves,
> Sea waves are my friends.
> When they become angry,
> Sea waves give the challenges.
> God has given the courage,
> To challenge the sea waves.
> And we will succeed,
> We will succeed
> With Almighty's grace.

All the members who were gathered in the village sang the poem with me and exhibited lots of courage and enthusiasm even though they had gone through severe suffering during the tsunami.

CONNECTIVITY FOR SOCIETAL TRANSFORMATION

I addressed the Pan-African Parliament on 16 September 2004 in Johannesburg, South Africa. This was attended by fifty-three member countries of the African Union. I proposed the concept of a Pan-African e-network for providing seamless and integrated satellite, fibre optics and wireless network connecting fifty-three African countries at an estimated cost of US $100 million.

As part of the project twelve universities (seven from India and five from Africa), seventeen super specialty hospitals (twelve from India and five from Africa), fifty-three tele-medicine centres and fifty-three tele-education centres in Africa will be connected. The pilot project on tele-education and tele-medicine in Ethiopia has already been commissioned. The Indira Gandhi National Open University has taken up MBA courses for thirty-four Ethiopian students of Addis Ababa and Harmaya Universities. As regards tele-medicine, the specialists from CARE Hospital, Hyderabad have been providing one-hour live tele-consultation to doctors in Black Lion Hospital, Addis Ababa, in cardiology and radiology since November 2006. Using the Pan-African network the heads of the state all the fifty-three countries will be connected for instant communication. I am extremely happy that Indian experience in bringing the benefits of technology to people has enabled us to work with Africa to bring societal transformation in the African continent.

DEFENDING THE NATION

I visited the Kumar post on the Siachen Glacier located at 17,000 feet above sea level held by the Indian Army, had a memorable underwater journey in INS *Sindhurakshak* and flew in a Sukhoi-30 fighter experiencing 2.5 Gs. In these three experiences, I personally felt proud of our ever-vigilant soldiers, sailors and air warriors performing tasks beyond the call of their duty even in the most adverse circumstances, both natural and manmade. During the last five years, I had an opportunity to present colours to many regiments, participate in a number of passing-out parades, meet troops who were going to undertake peace-keeping missions and interact with the family members of our defence forces. Our defence forces are in a beautiful mission. When the nation sleeps members of our defence teams are awake to guard us and remain vigilant to counter any threat. The nation cherishes the valour, commitment and devotion to duty of our defence forces. Similarly, I had opportunities to interact with members of our para-military forces, central and state police personnel, including internal security forces who are making immense contributions in augmenting the safety and security of our citizens under difficult conditions.

YOUTH MOVEMENT FOR DEVELOPED INDIA 2020

Recently, in Hyderabad, I met a group of citizens who are putting into practice the motto of transforming of our youth into enlightened citizens. The Lead India 2020 Foundation created by Dr N.B. Sudershan at Hyderabad is training thousands of students in many districts of Andhra Pradesh in partnership with the district administration. Particularly, I happened to know the transformation which has taken place among the students of the Medak district. As per the district authorities, the impact of the training on the students is visible in terms of self-discipline, love for their parents and teachers shedding of stage fear and recognition of their duties towards the nation. I talked to Ms Padma, a student leader from Andhra Pradesh Tribal Welfare School, Nalgonda, who related how she weaned her father away from smoking after imbibing the spirit of the ten-point oath from the Lead India Training Camp. This gives me an assurance that the youth of our country are on the right path through this mission-oriented programme. With the ignited minds of the 540 million youth below the age of twenty-five, which I consider is the most powerful resource on the earth, under the earth and above the earth, we have to empower the youth through value-based education and leadership.

CONCLUSION

I was touched by the variety of Indian panorama, emotional content of the tune, cultural diversity and unity of minds in the vast land of ours. I have cited these examples just to give a glimpse of the richness of our tradition and effort being taken by different agencies to preserve it. There are also many new adventures by institutions and individuals. I have experienced many of them and learnt a lot about my country and our people. Even while pursuing our economic growth, we need to do a lot to preserve the rich and diverse treasures of our culture and civilization. It is our duty for our future generations. This has to be done in a much larger scale through countrywide participation of multiple institutions. Our country is blessed with natural resources, has shown considerable progress in the last sixty years and, above all, we have hardworking people, particularly the power of the 540 million youth of the country. Every sector of our country has given me the confidence that India can become a developed nation well before 2020. Whomsoever I meet constantly ask what they can give to the nation. We should constantly strive to empower such members of the society. With this spirit, I am extremely happy that we are on the right path. Here I am reminded of a famous poem:

When you wish upon a star,
Makes no difference who you are,
Anything your heart desires,
Will come to you?

This poem is true to all of us, and particularly for our youth and if they aim great, I am sure they will reach close to the target or the target itself.

My dear citizens, let us resolve to continue to work for realizing the missions of developed India 2020 with the following distinctive profile.

1. A nation where the rural and urban divide has reduced to a thin line.

2. A nation where there is an equitable distribution and adequate access to energy and quality water.

3. A nation where agriculture, industry and service sector work together in symphony.

4. A nation where education with value system is not denied to any meritorious candidates because of societal or economic discrimination.

5. A nation which is the best destination for the most talented scholars, scientists and investors.

6. A nation where the best of health care is available to all.

7. A nation where the governance is responsive, transparent and corruption free.
8. A nation where poverty has been totally eradicated, illiteracy removed and crimes against women and children are absent and no one in the society feels alienated.
9. A nation that is prosperous, healthy, secure, peaceful and happy and continues with a sustainable growth path.
10. A nation that is one of the best places to live in and is proud of its leadership.

Finally, let me thank each one of you for showering your love and affection on me throughout the last five years by your cooperation and support.

Dear citizens, I conclude my address by sharing with you my mission in life which is to bring connectivity between billion hearts and minds of the people of India in our multicultural society and to embed the self confidence that 'we can do it'. I will be always with you, dear citizens, in the great mission of making India a developed nation before 2020.

May God bless you.

Jai Hind.

Meeting Young Minds

*Keep asking questions till
you get satisfactory answers.*

Give Us a Role Model

Men often become what they believe themselves to be. If I believe
I cannot do something, it makes me incapable of doing it. But
when I believe I can, then I acquire the ability to do it even if
I didn't have it in the beginning.

—Mahatma Gandhi

WHY SHOULD I meet young students in particular? Seeking the answer I went back to my student days. From the island of Rameswaram, what a great journey it's been! Looking back it all seems quite incredible. What was it that made it possible? Hard work? Ambition? Many things come to my mind. I feel the most important thing was that I always assessed my worth by the value of my contribution. The fundamental thing is that you must know that you deserve the good things of life, the benefits that God bestows. Unless our students and young believe that they are worthy of being citizens of a developed India, how will they ever be responsible and enlightened citizens?

There is nothing mysterious about the abundance in developed nations. The historic fact is that the people of these nations—the G8 as they are called—believed over many generations that they must live a good life in a strong and prosperous nation. The reality became aligned with their aspirations.

I do not think that abundance and spirituality are mutually exclusive or that it is wrong to desire material things. For instance, while I personally cherish a life with minimum of possessions, I admire abundance, for it brings along with it security and confidence, and these eventually help preserve our freedom. Nature, too, does not do anything by half measures, as you will see if you look around you.

213

Go to a garden. In season, there is a profusion of flowers. Or look up. The universe stretches into infinitude, vast beyond belief.

All that we see in the world is an embodiment of energy. We are a part of the cosmic energy too, as Sri Aurobindo says. Therefore when we begin to appreciate that spirit and matter are both part of existence, are in harmony with each other, we shall realize that it is wrong to feel that it is somehow shameful or non-spiritual to desire material things.

Yet, this is what we are often led to believe. Certainly there is nothing wrong with an attitude of making do with the minimum, in leading a life of asceticism. Mahatma Gandhi led such a life but in his case as in yours it has to be a matter of choice. You follow such a lifestyle because it answers a need that arises from deep within you. However, making a virtue of sacrifice and what is forced upon you—to celebrate suffering—is a different thing altogether. This was the basis of my decision to contact our young. To know their dreams and tell them that it is perfectly all right to dream of a good life, an abundant life, a life full of pleasures and comforts, and work for that golden era. Whatever you do must come from the heart, express your spirit, and thereby you will also spread love and joy around you.

My first such meeting took place in a high school in Tripura. It was a gathering of 500 students and teachers. After my talk on the second vision for transforming India into a developed nation, there were a series of questions, two of which I would like to discuss. The first question was: 'Where do we get a role model from, how do you get a role model?'

Whether we are aware of it or not, from childhood onwards, through various phases of life, we adopt role models. I said, 'When you are growing up, say till the age of fifteen, the best role model I can think of would be your father, your mother and your school teacher.' They, to my mind, are the people who can impart the best guidance during this period. I turned to the teachers and parents present there and told them what a big responsibility they have. I personally believe the full development of a child with a value system can only come from these people. In my own home, when I was growing up, I used to see my father and mother say namaz five times a day, and in spite of their modest financial resources, I found them always giving to the needy around. My teacher, Sivasubramania Iyer, was responsible for persuading my father to send me to school setting aside financial constraints. It is very important for every parent to be willing to make the effort to guide children to be good human beings—enlightened and hard-working. The teacher, the child's window to learning and knowledge, has to play the role model in generating creativity in the child. This triangle is indeed the real role model I can think of. I would even go to the extent of saying that if parents and teachers show the required dedication to shape the lives of the young, India would get a new life. As it is said: Behind the parents stands the school, and behind the teacher the home. Education and the teacher-student relationship have to be seen not in business terms but with the nation's growth in mind. A proper education would help nurture a sense of dignity and self-respect among our youth. These are qualities no law can enforce—they have to be nurtured ourselves.

The children enjoyed this answer though I don't know whether the parents and teachers got the message.

Another girl in all seriousness asked, 'Every day we read in the newspaper or hear our parents talk about atankvadis (terrorists). Who are they? Do they belong to our country?' This question really shocked me. I myself was searching for an answer. They are our own people. Sometimes we create them through political and economic isolation. Or they can be fanatics, sometimes sponsored by hostile nations, trying to disrupt normal life through terrorism. I looked at the audience, at the people sitting by my side, at the teachers, and at the sky for an answer. I said, 'Children, I am reminded of our epics, the Ramayana and Mahabharata. In the Ramayana the battle is between the divine hero Rama and demon king Ravana. It is a long-drawn battle that finally Rama wins. In the Mahabharata, there is the battle at Kurukshetra. In this fight between good and evil, Dharma wins again. The battles are many but finally peace triumphs. In our times, too, we have seen this battle between good and evil—for instance, the Second World War. It seems to me that both good and evil will survive side by side. The

Almighty does help them both to various degrees! How to minimize the evil through our spiritual growth is a question that has persisted throughout human history.'

On another occasion, I addressed a very large gathering of students at St. Mary's School, Dindigul in Tamil Nadu on their seventy-fifth anniversary celebrations. Among the large number of children wishing to meet me were two who were in a hurry to get an answer from me. One student asked, 'I have read your book *Agni Siragugal* (the Tamil version of *Wings of Fire*). You always give a message to dream. Tell me, why dream?'

My answer was to ask the gathered children to recite the following: 'Dream, dream, dream. Dream transforms into thoughts. Thoughts result in actions.' I told them, 'Friends, if there are no dreams, there are no revolutionary thoughts; if there are no thoughts, no actions will emanate. Hence, parents and teachers should allow their children to dream. Success always follows dreams attempted though there may be some setbacks and delays.'

Another boy asked, 'Please tell me, who would be the first scientist in the world?' It occurred to me—science was born and survives only by questions. The whole foundation of science is questioning. And as parents and teachers well know, children are the source of unending questions. Hence, 'Child is the first scientist,' I replied. There was thunderous applause. The children enjoyed this different way of thinking. Teachers and parents also smiled at the answer.

During my visit to Assam, I visited Tezpur. I had gone for the convocation ceremony of Tezpur University and also to receive the honorary doctorate conferred on me. After the convocation, I took off to meet schoolchildren. It was a big gathering of young people. The theme of my address was 'Indomitable Spirit'. As soon I finished my talk the youngsters mobbed me for autographs. When I finished giving autographs I faced two interesting questions. One was: 'Why cannot water from the Brahmaputra, which is in flood much of the time, be diverted to Rajasthan or Tamil Nadu which are starved of water?'

Only children will have these innovative ideas. Grown-ups tend to see more impossibilities. It was such a powerful question, I was completely beaten. I was sure even the prime minister would not have been able to answer it! How to tell the boy, rivers are a state subject and our states are fighting for the rights to their waters? That these would bring them prosperity some day but meanwhile they were flowing wastefully into the sea and causing floods every year. How to answer it?

I said, 'India Vision 2020 demands from the young that they start a great mission of connecting rivers cutting across the states.' I personally feel the young have the most powerful minds. They can overcome the negativity of the bureaucracy and some self-centred policies of the state governments to enrich the people of the country. They can even improve coordination between the states and the Centre. And they surely will!

Another student asked me a question for which again I had no ready answer. He said. 'Sir, big leaders in any field don't come and talk to us. We see our prime minister often going to Chennai, Lucknow, and many places. But he never comes here. We want him; we want to talk to him.' I was impressed by this urge to communicate with the country's leaders. I said, when I reach Delhi, I will tell your dream to the leaders and your dream will come true.

I later narrated this to the prime minister. He conceded the point and said, 'Children don't talk to me any more. Maybe the security cordon has created a separation. I request our leaders in different fields to interact more with the children of the country for a better understanding of their own purpose in life as also for helping create a better future for our children.'

I have visited Jharkhand a number of times after its formation. Every time I visit it, I am struck by the tremendous resources that wait to be harnessed in the state, which will multiply its wealth manifold. At the Sri Ramakrishna High School, Bokaro, I addressed a gathering of about 3,000 students and saw their creativity on display in an exhibition of their paintings, toys and other items made by them. In my conversation with them, one student asked me, 'In Jharkhand, it is green everywhere. We have forests, streams and hills. Why is it that we have a desert in Rajasthan?'

The question reminded me of a similar one in Assam: Why cannot the Brahmaputra's waters be taken to Tamil Nadu and Rajasthan? 'You know, twenty years ago, you would not have seen much cultivation in Rajasthan. But once the Indira Gandhi Canal was constructed agriculture became possible in many places. It is possible for man to transform the desert into a fertile land.' I repeated what I had told the student in Assam. 'It has to be one of the greatest missions of India to connect rivers so that water can reach many water-starved states. Visionary action is needed. When you grow up you will probably be part of reconstructing this nation and giving shape to these thoughts.'

One child came to me with a serious expression and asked, 'Sir, will your Agni missile cross the ocean and reach America?'

I was a little startled by this thought. 'For us no country is our enemy to send Agni there. Particularly, America is our friend. Agni symbolizes our strength. It shows that India has all the capabilities.'

During my visit to Cuttack I participated in the birthday celebrations of the late Justice Harihar Mahapatra. I went there at the invitation of Justice Ranganath Mishra. For me, it was a revelation, how the independence movement, the first vision for the nation, had created the larger-than-life figure of Justice Harihar Mahapatra. He lived to the age of ninety-two and established the Cuttack Eye Hospital, the Utkal University and 'above all' organized multi-pronged efforts to remove poverty. My biography in Oriya was released. At the end of my speech the youngsters crowding around put forth many questions.

The first question was, 'Sir, tell us which are your favourite books, that you loved and which have shaped your mind?'

I said, 'Four books in my life have been very close to my heart. I cherish reading them. The first is *Man the Unknown* by Dr Alexis Carrel, a doctor-turned-philosopher and a Nobel laureate. This book highlights how the mind and body both have to be treated in an ailment as the two are integrated. You cannot treat one and ignore the other. In particular, children who dream of becoming doctors should read the book. They will learn that the human body is not a mechanical system; it is a very intelligent organism with a most intricate and sensitive feedback system. The second book, one I venerate, is Tiruvalluvar's *Thirukkural*, which provides an excellent code of life. The third is *Light from Many Lamps* by Lillian Eichler Watson which has touched me deeply. It illuminates how we live and has been an invaluable guide to me for fifty years. And the Holy Koran is, of course, a constant companion.'

While I was addressing another gathering of schoolchildren in Anand, Gujarat, one smart boy asked a very intelligent question: 'Who is our enemy?' I liked the question and put it to the other students, encouraging them to come forward with their views. Then came the answer, 'Poverty.' What a wise reaction!

The last question, which I am including here, came from the powerful mind of another child. 'Tell me, sir, are Pakistani weapons stronger than Indian ones?' I asked the child why this doubt arose in his mind. Reports he read in the media led him to think so, he said.

'This is a unique characteristic of our country—to belittle our capabilities. It may even be genetic!' I said. 'India can design, develop and produce any type of missile and any type of nuclear weapon. This is a capability only four countries in the world have. You remove all the doubts from your mind,' I told the child, who gave me a very satisfied look.

I have selected only eleven questions here from among the hundreds of questions I have been asked during the course of meeting 40,000 high school students so far. The questions reflect the children's innocence, but most of all they show how strongly they feel the desire to live in a strong and prosperous nation. I also realized from these sessions how important it is for them to have role models, whether in science, industry, sports, entertainment or some other field. The question is: Can we give our children a role model? And how?

At the dawn of the new millennium came the news that the human genome had been decoded. All the 30,000 genes that human beings carry today, we are told, are identical to those of our Stone Age ancestors who lived thousands of years ago. One of the traits that has come down to us from them, along with others that are needed for survival, is the desire for achievement.

It is said that nature gave us this instinct because the need to achieve, like the need to reproduce, the need to eat, the need to drink and the need to breathe, is simply too important to be left to chance. History shows the hunger for achievement is a highly evolved one and undoubtedly the strongest one. We tend to forget it but it underlines much of our experience. Most important, without it, how would we learn and grow, aspire to greater perfection?

I have seen Prof. Vikram Sarabhai's vision succeeding over three decades through sustained and coordinated achievement. At work in that and any other endeavour was this same desire to exceed the limits. As we try and excel, role models play a guiding role. The power of Vikram Sarabhai was such that others took up his vision and completed it long after he was no more. For you it could be someone else whom you admire—a sportsperson, a teacher, a successful entrepreneur.

I recently had the chance to meet a legendary personality, a role model herself. Lata Mangeshkar was presiding over a function in remembrance of her father, Master Deenanath Mangeshkar. Lata Mangeshkar is a recipient of the Bharat Ratna and I felt honoured that she had asked me to inaugurate the 450-bed Deenanath Hospital and Research Centre in Pune. I visited the hospital just before the inauguration. I found that it would be treating nearly 30 per cent of the patients free. I was touched by the fact that despite her wealth and fame, she had not lost sight of the fact that one needs to do all one can to help relieve the suffering of others.

Her songs played over the radio have brought pleasure to countless hearts over the decades. During the India-China conflict in 1962, her song 'Ae mere vatan ke logo' moved an entire nation. Few people can claim to have influenced the lives of millions in such a delightful way.

Role models can help us focus on what is correct for us as individuals, as groups and, of course, as a nation. They can also lead us to great success. We seem to have got carried away with the success of a few in the field of information technology. But that is indeed nothing compared to what we can and should achieve. Ancient India was a knowledge society and a leader in many intellectual pursuits, particularly in the fields of mathematics, medicine and astronomy. A renaissance is imperative for us to once again become a knowledge superpower rather than simply providing cheap labour in areas of high technology.

Conversations

In your opinion, who serves untry best—a soldier, a teacher, a doctor, a scientist or a politician?
—Tarannum, Kendriya Vidyalaya, Pathankot

All have their own role to play to serve the country in the best possible way.

A soldier has to defend the nation and keep round-the-clock vigil so that a billion-plus people can work towards development in peace.

A teacher has to create enlightened citizens and future leaders.

'Use your brain to remove the pain of suffering humanity' should be the motto of doctors.

Scientists should provide the inputs needed for achieving development.

Politicians have to integrate and guide the actions of all sections of the community towards a common goal of national development.

And above all one has to be a good human being.

55 per cent of the Indian population comprises of the youth and we all believe in the energy of the youth. My question is—what is the role of the youth of India in active politics?
—Tushar Katyayan, Siddaganga Institute of Technology, Tumkur

The youth have to exercise their vote to ensure the success of those candidates who focus on the development of the nation. Educating people about the right and wrong candidate should be an important mission for the youth. So far I have met over five million youth and in each forum I have asked, how many people will join politics? The number who want to join politics is slowly increasing. I would like to share with you some of the very typical answers I got in response to my question—why do you want to join politics? A girl from Jalandhar said that her main aim in joining politics was to remove casteism in the country. A girl from Lucknow said that she would promote the vision of the nation and transform the vision into missions and projects for time-bound development of the nation.

What kind of future do you foresee for the Indian youth?
—Mueen Farooq Hakak, St. George College, Mussoorie

We have 540 million young people in our country. This is our core strength. They should contribute to transforming India into a developed nation. They should study well and excel. Entrepreneurship training should become part of their education. They should all aim to become employment generators rather than employment seekers. Great responsibilities are waiting for you, such as networking of rivers, execution of PURA, and, above all, transforming India into a developed nation. Every action that you do, you have to keep in mind our major mission of transforming India into a developed nation.

What changes should be made in the present education system so that the students of science feel more enthusiastic about the study of science?
—Huda Masood, Sr Sec. School, Aligarh

Firstly, the simple beauty of logic in science should be explained to the students. Take the example of our human body. Science has revealed that the human body is made up of millions and millions of atoms. An average adult weighing 70 kilogrammes would have approximately 7×10^{27} atoms, that is, 7 followed by twenty-seven zeros. For example, I am made up of 5.8×10^{27} atoms. These are further divided into 4.7×10^{27} hydrogen atoms, another 1.5×10^{27} oxygen atoms, and there are 47.5×10^{26} carbon atoms. The difference between one human being and another is determined by the sequencing of the atoms. Such beauty of science should be explained to the students. Secondly, we must have inspiring teachers in science. Thirdly, students must be exposed to the lives and work of great scientists, so that they can derive inspiration from them. Fourthly, the value of science must be emphasized by senior scientists.

Recently, I was reading *The Big and the Small: From the Microcosm to the Macrocosm* by Dr G. Venkataraman. In this book, the author establishes a fascinating link between particles of physics and cosmology. I would like to narrate an incident from the book about Sir C.V. Raman. Raman was in the first batch of Bharat Ratna Award winners. The award ceremony was to take place in the last week of January, soon after the Republic Day celebrations of 1954. The then President, Dr Rajendra Prasad, wrote to Raman inviting him to be his personal guest in the Rashtrapati Bhavan, when he came to Delhi for the award ceremony. Raman wrote a polite letter, regretting his inability to do so. And he had a noble reason for his inability to attend the investiture ceremony. He explained to the President that he was guiding a Ph.D student and that the thesis had to be submitted by the last day of January. The student was valiantly trying to wrap it up and Raman felt he had to be by the side of the research student to see that the thesis was finished, sign the thesis as the guide and then have it submitted. Here was a scientist who gave up the pomp of a glittering ceremony associated with the highest honour, because he felt that his duty required him to be by the side of the student. It is this character that truly builds science. Students must be encouraged to build such character.

Please give some message of inspiration to all of us.
—Jyoti, D.A.V. School, Chandigarh

I have a message for the youth of our country. All the youth should have indomitable spirit. Indomitable spirit has two components. First, you should have an aim and then work hard for it. Second, while working, you will definitely encounter some problems. In those circumstances, do not allow problems to become your master, instead you should become master of the problems, defeat them and succeed. Fortunately, our nation has a great resource of young population. Ignited minds of the young are the greatest resource compared to any other resource. When ignited minds work and perform with an indomitable spirit, a prosperous, happy and safe India is assured.

Acknowledgements

Grateful acknowledgement is made to the following for permission to reprint copyright material.

'Wings of Fire', 'Into the World of Rocketry', 'Teachers and Awards', 'Light Up the Sky', '"I Am a Well In This Great Land" ' are excerpted from *Wings of Fire: An Autobiography*, A.P.J. Abdul Kalam with Arun Tiwari, Universities Press, 1999.

'Three Great Hearts Resolve a Problem', 'My Mother and My Sister', 'My Mentor; Dr Vikram Sarabhai' are excerpted from *My Journey: Transforming Dreams Into Actions*, A.P.J. Abdul Kalam, Rupa Publications, 2013

'A Conversation' is excerpted from *Guiding Souls: Dialogues on the Purpose of Life*, A.P.J. Abdul Kalam with Arun K. Tiwari, Ocean Books, 2005

'Seven Turning Points of My Life', 'The Interactive President' are excerpted from *Turning Points: A Journey Through Challenges*, A.P.J. Abdul Kalam, HarperCollins *Publishers* India, 2012. Reproduced by arrangement with HarperCollins *Publishers* India Limited. Unauthorized copying is strictly prohibited.

'The Message in the Cave' is excerpted from *Squaring the Circle: Seven Steps to Indian Renaissance*, A.P.J. Abdul Kalam with Arun Tiwari, Universities Press, 2013

'Five Mighty Souls', 'Abiding Values' are excerpted from *Indomitable Spirit*, A.P.J. Abdul Kalam, Rajpal & Sons, 2011

'The Knowledge Society', 'Give Us a Role Model' are excerpted from *Ignited Minds: Unleashing the Power Within India*, A.P.J. Abdul Kalam, Penguin Books India, 2002

'Creative Leadership: The Essence of Good Governance', 'E-governance for Transparent Societies', 'The Effects of Corruption',

'The Vision for a New India' are excerpted from *Governance for Growth In India*, A.P.J. Abdul Kalam, Rupa Publications India, 2014

'Conversations' is excerpted from *Spirit of India*, A.P.J. Abdul Kalam, Rajpal & Sons, 2010

'The Joy of Reading' is based on the address at the 11th National Book Fair, Lucknow, 27 September 2013

'Education Enhances the Dignity of Human Life' is based on the lecture given to the teachers of Anna University, Chennai on Teacher's Day, 2014

'The Environment Challenge' is based on the address at the inauguration of the 10th Kerala Environment Congress and Shri M.R. Kurup Memorial Keynote address, 22 August 2014.